Voices
OF RWANDA

JAM International

Copyright © 2003, JAM International

JAM International
P.O. Box 1502, Honeydew 2040
South Africa
Tel: +27 (11) 548-3900, Fax: +27 (11) 548-3996/7
Website: www.jamint.com

ISBN: 1 904722 01 6

Designed & Published by:
Camerapix Publishers International
P.O Box 45048, Nairobi, Kenya
Tel: 254-2 4448923/4/5,
Fax: 254-2 4448926/7
Email: camerapix@iconnect.co.ke

Printed and bound: Singapore.

Acknowledgements

Jean Paul Byiringiro (Translation, locating of orphans and liaison)

Jean Claude Rukundo (Translation and locating of orphans in Kigali)

Joshua and Neena Irshad (Management: Fred Nkunda Life Centre)

Doreen Nkunda (Management: Fred Nkunda Life Centre)

The Byiringiro family

John Basomingera (Locating of Orphans in Bisesero)

The Basomingera family

All who helped us locate ex-JAM orphans

All the staff at Fred Nkunda Life Centre

Heidi Westli (Interviews and editing)

Gaute Westli (photography)

Johan Etsebeth (Interviews, editing, photography)

Craig Bredenkamp, Ann Pretorius, Candice Pretorius (editing)

All the schools that allowed us to do interviews

The Pentecostal Church in Kibuye for Accommodation —
Ruth, Celestine and Augustine

A.D.E.P.R. Mission in Kigali for Accommodation

The Rwandan Police and Police Commander in Kibuye

All ex-JAM orphans who agreed to share their stories

All those we have neglected to mention, but without whom the
execution of this project could not have been possible

The friendly citizens of Rwanda

Preface

It was 1994. Media reports covered the awful atrocities of The Rwandan Genocide.

I knew I could call on James Robison, my faithful friend with whom I had worked for many years in alleviating poverty in Africa, to meet me in Rwanda to assess the situation. We found Fred Nkunda, a man with a heart and determination much larger than his meagre finances. We knew that together we could do much for these precious children, victims of a man-made disaster.

With the help of friends from all over the world, we have been able to take care of thousands of these children, build a facility which at times bursts at its seams with over 700 children, and enjoy seeing the wonderful results in their lives.

This is the reason for the book — to share with you the full joy and reality of what has happened in the lives of so many children whose voices need to be heard. They were in a hopeless situation, yet now have hope and dreams for the future.

I owe a debt of deep gratitude to these orphans of Rwanda. They brought a new dimension to my life — of understanding hope in a hopeless situation, of knowing what true courage really is, and understanding the meaning of trust and love. These children trusted us in a way that is difficult to comprehend, knowing they had been through such terrible situations. They opened their hearts to us and loved us like father and mother, so affectionate and loving. Rwanda has a very special place in my heart.

I want to express my thanks to Mrs Aloisea Inyumba, who was the Rwandan Minister of Social Affairs, and who worked so closely with us to care for these children; James and Betty Robison who partnered with us in the truest sense; and all the staff at the Rwanda Orphanage and the team of JAM International, who have given so much of themselves. Most of all, Fred Nkunda, who died in 1996 while running the orphanage — a man with a big heart; and Fred's wife, Doreen Nkunda, who today continues to work as a manager at this orphanage.

Peter Pretorius
Founder / CEO
JAM International

Foreword

What Betty and I have witnessed working alongside Peter and Ann Pretorius can only be attributed to the supernatural power of love — God's love. This love is released through yielded human vessels. The impact is transforming in its effect, now and forever.

Voices of Rwanda contains just a few glimpses of the glory revealed through the lives of those who have experienced this indescribable power. The individuals you will read about have been raised from the ashes of pain, suffering, destruction and the death of many loved ones to discover hope, life and the opportunity of releasing the love they have received.

These stories would have been impossible to share without the prayers and financial support of caring people who wish to have a part in expressing the heart of God and extending His hands of compassion. Thank you for blessing others.

James Robison
Founder and President
Life Outreach International
Fort Worth, Texas
U.S.A

Surrounded by orphans from left to right Ann Pretorius, Betty Robison, James Robison and Peter Pretorius.

Message from the Governor of Kigali

In 1994 Rwanda experienced one of the worst cases of genocide in modern times when more than 800,000 people were killed. The social effects on Rwandan society were severe, for the conflict left behind a highly traumatized population with between 350,000 and 400,000 orphans and a situation where one-third of Rwandan households are now headed by widows.

When the Government of National Unity took over in July 1994, one of the main challenges was to rebuild the social fabric which had been destroyed.

At the Ministry of Gender and Social Affairs, one of our main partners who worked with us successfully in meeting these challenges was JAM International, specifically through the JAM Orphanage in Gitarama Province.

In this orphanage the children received care, love and affection. Today the majority of these orphans have been fostered by different families, irrespective of their ethnic background.

I would like to thank Peter Pretorius who, through his passionate concern for these children, ensured that they received adequate support through JAM International programmes which led to their successful reintegration into society.

The testimonies of these children, carefully compiled in this book, testify in a most vivid way to the tragedy that our country has gone through, but even more importantly, the hope of peace and reconciliation that lies ahead in our country.

Aloisea Inyumba
Formerly Minister of Gender & Social Affairs

Message from Ann Pretorius

Shocked by what we heard, yet encouraged by the relationship with James and Betty Robison who had partnered with us in many projects in African nations, we set out to provide a home for the orphans of Rwanda. They benefited but I believe we gained more — our lives have been enriched by theirs.

My husband, Peter, has often asked a question of our own six children: "What is your story?" It has always invited open communication and resulted in many 'heart-to-heart' chats. This is the same question asked of hundreds of children who witnessed atrocities beyond belief before they were brought to our orphanage.

I have had the privilege of working hand-in-hand with my husband, our partners, donors and staff in the establishment of a 'home' for these orphans. Although it could accommodate a maximum of 700 children, thousands have been through this facility before being placed in suitable homes. The greatest impact for me was to fall in love with these children and see the resilience and hope in their hearts. Hopefully this book has captured this, so it can be transferred to each reader.

I have observed that tough experiences do not kill us; they give us an opportunity to look ahead, define our dreams and pursue them. This strong thread of hope for a better future is a common positive attribute in these children. Many of them are now fostered into homes of relatives or placed with suitable parents in Rwanda.

With great admiration, we thank Heidi and Gaute Westli, Johan Etsebeth, and the translators Jean Paul Byiringiro and Jean Claude Rukundo who travelled throughout Rwanda, eight years after the awful genocide of 1994, to meet these children and capture their stories. Along with my daughter-in-law, Candice Pretorius, they have worked tirelessly to compile this book.

I believe these stories will change your life and alter your values.

Ann Pretorius
Assistant CEO
JAM International

Message from Isak Pretorius

The Rwandan Genocide of 1994 was one of the greatest atrocities to face the continent of Africa. Unfortunately those hardest hit were the children. Young lives were thrown into turmoil as many of them witnessed the brutal killing of their parents. These children were left to fend for themselves, wandering in forests, stealing food and fighting to stay alive! Many of these children have come through JAM's Orphanage in Gitarama, and when asked how they felt about what they have been through, they expressed only forgiveness and their longing for a safe and united Rwanda. It is these children that have given the nation hope, hope that reconciliation and true unity is possible.

The incredible forgiveness and total lack of revenge shown by the children in our orphanage has been what has motivated us to write this book. A book that tells heart-breaking stories of what children have been through and yet each story has a common theme: a fight for survival and a heart of forgiveness and a hope for tomorrow.

The research for the book was done by four JAM staff members over a three-month period. The process was difficult as permission had to be obtained from the children, their guardians or foster families and the relevant authorities. Large distances needed to be covered, very often on bad roads, and the team faced a traumatizing experience each time they spoke to a new child. The children themselves would very often almost relive the trauma of what they had been through as they told their stories.

I believe that a united Rwanda is possible and that a genocide need never happen again, because I have seen and experienced first hand the forgiveness of the children whose stories are in this book. Stories that are there to remind us of how evil humanity can be and yet, at the same time, to show that this can all be changed if we take our example from the children of Rwanda.

Isak Pretorius
Chief Operating Officer
JAM International

The Rwandan Flag – Old and New

NEW SYMBOLISM IN RWANDA

H. E. Paul Kagame, President of the Republic of Rwanda, unveiled new national symbols for Rwanda on 31 December 2001. Rwanda's old flag, national anthem and coat of arms were replaced by new symbolism that is not associated with struggle and conflict, as before. Rwanda's old national symbols were steeped in the country's bloody history of genocide and revolution between the country's three tribes, the Hutu, Tutsi and Twa.

The new anthem and flag represents Rwandans as one nation, signifying work, patriotism and hope for the future. It was designed by Alphonse Kirimobenecyo, a Rwandan artist and engineer.

The colours of the old Rwandan flag were red, yellow and green with a black letter 'R' for Rwanda in the centre. The new flag does not contain the colours of red and black with their connotations of blood and darkness. The top half of the new flag is blue with the sun in the top right-hand corner. Blue signifies peace and tranquility, yellow wealth as the country works toward sustainable economic growth and green symbolizes prosperity, work and productivity. The image of the sun signifies new hope, and its light signifies transparency.

Rwanda is on its way to reconciliation and unity, and serves as an example to the rest of the world how a nation can rise from the ashes of the worst humanitarian disaster in the late 20th century.

Information partly taken from the official website of the Republic of Rwanda: www.rwanda1.com

RWANDA

- ·—··— International boundary
- ·—·—· Prefecture boundary
- ——— Road
- - - - - Track
- ✪ National capital
- ⊙ Prefecture capital
- ○ Town

UGANDA

DEMOCRATIC
REPUBLIC OF THE
CONGO

Kafunzo
Merama
Kagitumba
Rwemhasha
Lubirizi
Rutshuru
Kisoro
Cyanika
Kabale
Nyagatare
Butaro
Muvumba
Kidaho
Katuna
Mulindi
Gatunda
KAGERA
Rwanyakizinga
Ngarama
Lac Mikindi
Ruhengeri
Kirambo
BYUMBA
Gabiro
NATIONAL
Lac Hago
Kora
Busogo
Cyamba
Byumba
Mutura
RUHENGERI
Lac Ruhondo
Kinihira
Kagali
Nemba
Kinyami
Muhura
Lac Kivumba
Goma
Gisenyi
Rukara
PARK
Nyundo
Rutare
Lac Ihema
Kabaya
Ngaru
Rushashi
Murambi
GISENYI
Mbogo
Shyorongi
Lac Muhazi
Ngororero
Kiyumba
KIGALI
Kinyinya
Gikoro
Lac Nasho
Rwamagana
Bulinga
Runda
Kigali
Kicukiro
Bicumbi
Kayonza
Lac Mpanga
Lac Cyambwe
Lake Bisongou
Butamwa
Mabanza
Gitarama
Kigarama
Kibuye
Birambo
GITARAMA
Bugesera
Kibungo
Rukira
Gishyita
Bwakira
Masango
Ruhango
Rilima
Sake
KIBUNGO
Rwamatamu
Gatagara
Gashora
Bare
Rusumo
Kaduha
Nyabisindu
Ngenda
Nemba
Kirehe
GIKONGORO
Karaba
Rusatira
Lac Cyohoha Sud
Rwesero
Karama
Ngenda
Kamembe
Gisakura
Gikongoro
Lac Rweru
Bukavu
Cyangugu
Rwumba
Kitabi
CYANGUGU
Karengera
Cyimbogo
Nyakabuye
Bugumya
Ruramba
Butare
Gisagara
BUTARE
BURUNDI
UNITED
REPUBLIC OF
TANZANIA
Bugarama
Muninio
Busoro
Runyombyi

The boundaries and names shown on this map do not imply
official endorsement or acceptance by the United Nations.

0   10   20   30 km
0   10   20 mi

Map No. 3717 Rev. 7   UNITED NATIONS
December 1997 (Colour)

Department of Public Information
Cartographic Section

Introduction to the Genocide and how JAM International and Life Outreach International became involved

(Taken from JAM archive material and 'History of a Genocide' by Gerard Prunier)

In 1994 the world received news of something terrible happening in a small country in the middle of Africa. Up to that year, people did not know much about Rwanda, but when the extent of this 'conflict' became known, people realized that genocide was taking place on a huge scale. By the end some 800,000 Tutsi were killed by groups of militia — the military and ordinary people that seized the opportunity to be part of this government-sanctioned slaughter. As with many African conflicts, it went relatively unnoticed until people realized the extent of this tragedy; it will remain like a blood stain on the pages of human history books.

Outcries came from far afield to stop the killings that everybody knew to be senseless. The genocide continued, for three months before it finally came to a halt with the RPA (Rwandan Patriotic Army) driving the militia out of the country and French troops guarding groups of Tutsi.

A country had been devastated. Corpses littered the lush, green hills and valleys and polluted the streams of this mountainous country. Rabid dogs roamed the empty streets and flocks of crows circled the sky. By this time almost everyone had fled the country in the confusion.

Small groups of people slowly emerged from squalid hiding places like ditches and the pits of toilets. People slowly started filtering back to Rwanda from the surrounding countries. Children were the ones worst hit. Lost, starved, diseased and traumatised they wandered around the forests, looking for roots and leaves to satisfy their hunger. The 'fortunate' ones were living in strangers' houses in strange countries and refugee camps. This had been a long journey for them.

Camps were established to gather groups of people together and humanitarian aid flooded into the country. A Ugandan man by the name of Fred Nkunda started gathering children from among the chaos in temporary IDP (Internally Displaced People) Camps.

JAM International went to Rwanda in August 1994 after working in the refugee camps of Goma in the Democratic Republic of Congo (then called Zaire). James Robison of Life Outreach International and Peter Pretorius of JAM International found Fred Nkunda, desperately trying to care for many orphans but in great financial need. A partnership was founded between JAM International and Life Outreach International to establish a permanent facility to help the Rwandan children.

The Rwandan Government provided 15 hectares of land on which to establish a permanent facility and contributions from all over the world helped to build an orphanage for the orphans of the genocide. Construction commenced in June 1996, but Fred Nkunda passed away due to ill health before the orphanage was completed. Today the orphanage is known as the Fred Nkunda Life Centre. The Centre, which comprises a clinic, dining hall, laundry, kitchen, administration block, staff quarters and two large dormitories, was designed to accommodate 600 orphans. Within a month it was bursting at the seams with more than 700 children.

Soon, Fred Nkunda Life Centre in Gitarama was the biggest orphanage in Rwanda and, because of its central location, was used as the preferred orphanage by many NGOs working in Rwanda. Many children are still being repatriated today from surrounding countries and brought to orphanages in Rwanda.

Today the orphanage houses around 300 children, as most have been relocated with families, and it has been partly converted to a technical training centre. Relocation and fostering programmes are in place to reunite orphans with relatives or foster children with new local parents.

The orphanage is now transitioning into a Training Centre which offers the children skills training in computers, pottery, woodwork, sewing, handcrafts and many other skills.

"If I were President..."

After the genocide in 1994 Athanase came to JAM's Fred Nkunda Life Centre where he was taken good care of. ***"They gave us food and clothes and were kind to us. I remember the supervisors who told us about God and who taught us to pray."***

After two years in the orphanage the IRC traced his relatives in Kibuye and took him to his family. He was sad to leave the orphanage, as he knew life would be hard outside and that he would miss his friends.

"It was difficult to go back home because everything reminded me about the war. Some children found the dead bodies of their family and they had to report it to the police to bury them. Some children even became crazy for a while after the war."

He remembers how soldiers with machetes killed his parents. He used to hide for days during the daylight hours. He not only saw militia burn houses, but even cut down the banana plants and pull vegetables from the ground.

During his first months at home he missed the safe environment of the orphanage and many times longed to go back.

Despite his difficult past, Athanase is determined to do something about his future. He loves school, especially the courses on religion and psychology. He would even like to go as far as becoming a social worker in the future and study at university.

His biggest wish is to become a leader in Rwanda or even the President. He thinks that it is important to encourage people to build good relationships, despite their different backgrounds. ***"If I become the President of Rwanda I will work hard to develop the country. I would first of all focus on helping the people to make good decisions for their lives. I would tell the teachers the importance of teaching the children about doing good things and to respect each other. Actually, when I listen to the radio I hear that they talk about how to help the less educated people to get to school. If I become a President I will follow up on that issue and I will focus on informing the Rwandan people about the importance of education."***

Athanase Havugimana
Age 15
Region: Bisesero.
Attends Mubuga Primary School, level 6.

"The earth is not fertile any more"

Yves is 18 years old and is currently studying to become a teacher at Esapan Secondary School. He lost most of his family during the genocide and came to JAM's Fred Nkunda Life Centre soon after the war. He shared his thoughts with us:

"I grew up in a big family in Kibuye, but when the war started we were separated. I was hiding with people I did not know and French soldiers came and took me to the JAM Orphanage. I did not believe that anyone from my family had survived until they told me that they had found my mother. I was so happy.

"Our house was burnt in the war and my mother does not have money to build a new house on our land. We are happy to stay with my uncle but my dream is to go back to my place of origin and build a new house there. In Rwanda it is not common for the son to stay with his mother when he is getting his own family; the son is supposed to live on the father's land. Before the war we were farmers and although we were not rich, we had a good life. We had cows to fertilise the land and always had good harvests which enabled us to get enough food for our family and to sell in the market.

Yves Bikorimana
Age 18
Attends Esapan Secondary School, level 2.

" I don't think that people can be happy as farmers in Rwanda today. The earth is not very fertile any more. Most of the animals were killed in the war. The young people want to study rather than become farmers because it is not easy to survive. Many young boys have decided to leave the countryside to go to the city because they are not interested in working hard for very little money, as a farmer.

"I have heard about many boys who become street boys when they arrive in the city, because it is difficult to get a job when you don't have an education. They have to live on what they can get hold of – stealing or begging.

"I have decided to become a teacher because it is fairly easy to get a job as a teacher in Rwanda and I want to work with children. I am excited about starting to teach and I want to give the children what my teachers and leaders have given me.

"I think it is very important to teach children discipline. Disciplined people will easily live together with people from different backgrounds and they won't create division between people. I think a major cause of the war was division and I see it as my responsibility to teach the children to respect each other.

"When I start working I hope that I will get a good life – to have rich land and many cows. I want to buy some animals and start working on my land. If possible I will even hire some people who can help me dig the land while I am working."

Epiphanie Nyiranzabahimana
Age 24
Born in Rwankuba Bisesero.
Married to Innocent Ndoreyabo with three children.
Completed P6 in 1995 while still in JAM.

"Rwanda has a good, bright future if people can be reconciled"

"I am happy to have a family, be married and have children. I feel very happy in my heart about my children. Children are a benefit for their parents. I am married to Innocent Ndoreyabo with three children.

"We don't get enough food. I wish for the sake of my children's futures that we can have money for them to go to school. If you go to school you are able to help yourself and you can also serve your country.

"I left the orphanage when I was reunited with my brother. I was happy to be back in the place where I came from. I thought that if I came here that I could get some school materials, but my older brother was also poor because he was handicapped after they cut him in the face and head with a machete. We built a shelter of grass and lived there, while trying to grow some vegetables.

"I feel sad when I remember the war. We were living under very bad conditions; we had nothing to eat or drink because all the rivers were full of blood and of the people who were killed. The houses were also destroyed so we were staying in the rain on the mountains.

"I remember how it was before the war. We had brothers and sisters and a life, but now everybody has become handicapped and there are no brothers and sisters around any more. If you are sick they could come to you and help you. It is lonely to be left behind.

"I wish that we had peace in our country. If people understand each other, they can live again like they were living before. Rwanda has a good, bright future if people can be reconciled.

"When I think about what happened, I become sad because everybody lost so much. I keep quiet and patient about things. I sometimes talk to my husband about how the things happened. It helps to share what happened because it is good for people to talk about what happened here, but it is not good to think about it when you are alone. It is something that you cannot forget, because it has taken away your whole family and your parents.

"Every time you try something and you fail, you say that if your parents were still alive they could have helped you. If you are sick, you remember that you had people who could help you. You even remember how you used to eat with other people. Now you eat and you do not have an appetite.

"Every time this thing comes to mind, we pray to God to protect us from another war happening again in Rwanda."

Driving ambition

Thomas lives with a family who were his neighbours before the war began. He is thankful and says *"I lost my real family in the war, but when I came to Gaspard and Monique I got a new family. I am very happy to stay with them and they treat me as if I am their own son."*

Thomas grew up in the countryside of Kibuye where his parents worked as farmers. When the war started his entire family was killed, leaving him with nowhere to go. *"I met Gaspard and hid together with him during the war. I followed him wherever he went and he protected me all the time."*

They survived the war together and both went to the Fred Nkunda Life Centre after the war. Fred helped him and made him feel at home. Thomas was very happy at this time as he was going to school and got everything that he needed. However, after a few years, he was relocated to an orphanage in Kibuye so that he could be close to his place of origin.

Thomas Habiyaremye
Age 22
Region: Karora, Murangara, Kibuye.
Works as a farmer.

He wrote letters to Gaspard who was working at Fred Nkunda Life Centre. *"I used to write to Gaspard telling him how much I missed him and how difficult I found life in Kibuye. Most of the children who came to the orphanage only stayed for a short while before they were either reunited with relatives in the area or became foster children. I was very lonely and Gaspard felt sorry for me. Since he knew me from before the war, he and his wife decided to take me into their family."* They all moved back to Gaspard's house in Kibuye where they started ploughing the land.

When Thomas finished primary school he started working on the land and looked after the animals with Gaspard. *"I like to work as a farmer because I live in the countryside and we have to work the land to survive but I dream of going back to school one day to complete my studies. Most of all I would like to become a driver or a mechanic. If I can, I would like to go to a driving school to get a permit or to a technical school to get a diploma. If you have some sort of qualification it is easier to get a job."*

He dreams of one day being able to build a house on the land where his family lived before the war. *"I want to get married and have children. We could all dig the land together and have our own animals. It would be nice to be able to take care of myself without having to live on others' charity."*

Confidence in the future

Esperance lives happily together with her younger sister and brother in her uncle's house in Bisesero. She is in Esapan Secondary School in Ngoma.

Esperance likes to study and has not yet decided what courses to do, but is very interested in law. She would like to work as an administrator in the Government to teach the Rwandan people about culture and a good way of living.

"I have been living in a bad culture of ethnic divisions. I want to teach others about a better culture in order to avoid more genocide. Rwanda will be a better country when people start looking at each other with respect and when they see other people as the same as themselves. Our society has changed a lot since the war. In the schools the students mingle together and all the students are given the same opportunities despite what tribe they belong to."

Esperance was badly hurt in the war and has chest problems, headaches and back pain as a result. *"I don't like it very much when the other students do sports and I have to sit and watch them. I used to love to play volleyball."*

Esperance is a bright young girl and has many plans for the future. She says that if she does not manage to finish her studies or become an administrator, she wants to start her own business. *"I want to contact the bank for a loan so that I can start a small shop in Bisesero. I would like to sell different kinds of food and things for the house. I want to help my uncle and aunt and support them economically because they have helped us so much and they treat us as their own family."*

Esperance Mukamana
Age 15
Region: Bisesero.
Attends Esapan Secondary School, level 1.

"Nobody ever told me the reasons..."

Edith lives with her sister and her cousin and his wife and attends secondary school in Kibuye. She is training to be a nurse.

"I remember that the war started one afternoon in April 1994. I was at home when I suddenly heard gunshots outside our house. When I peeked out of the window I saw soldiers killing people with pangas and other traditional arms.

"I was separated from my family and for the first two weeks I hid in bushes. One day a group of militia discovered my hiding place but I managed to escape before they caught me. I met a boy from my village and he took me to his house. His mother was very kind to me and told me that she would do her best to protect me from the soldiers.

"After a few days they told me that my parents had been killed. I was very sad but the war was going on and there was nothing I could do about it. I didn't believe that the war would ever finish.

"I think a lot about why the war happened as nobody ever told me the reasons. I think the adults don't want me to know what really happened because it was so terrible. That is why I never ask either.

"Many things were destroyed in the war and in some areas where many families used to live before the war there are only a few people left. Schools and hospitals have been forced to close down because of the lack of staff and equipment. I hope that we will have peace in the future so that the population can increase and the country will be built up again. If we give birth to more children they will grow up understanding each other and the country will be developed.

"I think that many people who lost their families in the war are still very hurt. However, I believe that reconciliation will happen in Rwanda if the criminals will ask for forgiveness.

"My biggest wish for the future is that we will have peace in our country and that I will have peace in my heart."

Edith Mukarugambwa
Age 16
Region: Mugozi, Rwamatamu, Rwanyunda.
Attends ESIM Secondary School, level 2.

"My biggest wish is to help the people in my area"

Madeleine told us that she likes to study because education is important in having a good life. She says, **"I don't like to dig the land. I would rather have a good job outside my home."**

She shares the importance of women going to school as they are more respected than the women who stay at home: **"In the past women were told to stay at home to cook and look after the children. Luckily this has changed and the new leaders encourage women to develop themselves and start working outside the home. I think that the men in the cities are happy about this development, but the men in the countryside still want their wives to stay at home and not study.**

"I wish to become either a doctor or a nurse because I don't like to see people suffering. My biggest wish is to help the people in my area, who suffer from malaria or other serious diseases."

During the genocide Madeleine suffered much: **"When the war started we stayed in our house. One day my sister went to the spring to get water and some soldiers killed her. My parents understood this war was not going to end and decided we must leave our house and seek refuge in the mountains.**

"I was hiding with my mother in some bushes but the militia discovered us and started beating us with sticks. My mother soon died and they hit me several times on my head until I fell down. They obviously believed I had died because they left me there. When I slowly got to my feet and looked around, I saw only dead bodies, many of them being my own family and relatives. I did not know what to do – I just wanted to cry."

Madeleine Nyirahabimana
Age 18
Region: Bisesero.
Attends Rwamatamu College, Secondary level 2.

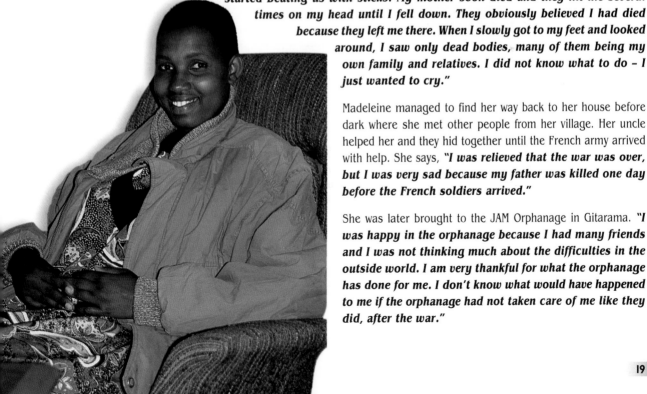

Madeleine managed to find her way back to her house before dark where she met other people from her village. Her uncle helped her and they hid together until the French army arrived with help. She says, **"I was relieved that the war was over, but I was very sad because my father was killed one day before the French soldiers arrived."**

She was later brought to the JAM Orphanage in Gitarama. **"I was happy in the orphanage because I had many friends and I was not thinking much about the difficulties in the outside world. I am very thankful for what the orphanage has done for me. I don't know what would have happened to me if the orphanage had not taken care of me like they did, after the war."**

"Education is important"

Anne Marie lives with her aunt and brother in Kigali because she lost her parents in the genocide in 1994. She shares her story with us:

"When the war started my family left the house and I was hiding with my mother and sisters after we got separated from my father and brother.

"During the day we were walking around trying to avoid the militia and at night we were sleeping wherever we could find a place to lie down. My mother used to take her clothes and spread them around her on the ground for us to sleep on. The only thing we ate was some bread that my mother bought for us every day, but I don't know if she ate anything herself. I never saw her eating anything.

"We kept going until we came to a church in town where many people were gathered. The militia came to the church and took people outside to kill them.

"My father was killed in the war and my mother died just after the war because of a disease. My brother, my sisters and I were relocated to the Fred Nkunda Life Centre where we lived for a couple of years before we were reunited with our aunt."

Anne Marie believes that the cause of the war was ignorance and lack of education. She thinks that by focusing on education, Rwanda will develop and become a good country to live in eventually: *"Education is important because students learn to live together and make good relationships. People should not stay ignorant, believing that if they kill a person they can take the property and land that belong to that man. The children should be taught about unity and reconciliation and they must learn that it is not good to divide people according to tribe. Education, together with love, will help people to respect each other. If the Rwandan people can come together and love each other I think that the country can develop and we will have peace at last."*

Anne Marie Dusabe
Age 15
Region: Karambo, Gatenga, Gikondo.
Attends Gikondo Primary School, level 6.

Happy to support her family

Pelagie finished her education in 1997 and was employed as a nurse in the local hospital in Gitarama. She married a few years later and laughs whilst sharing how she met her husband. *"It is normal for everybody to fall in love with someone. I met my husband in town and we started to like each other."*

Pelagie supports her six younger brothers and sisters with their studies. *"I am happy to help my family. Since I am educated and have a good job it is my duty to help them and support them economically."*

Her father and other brothers were killed at the beginning of the war. A few days after their death the militia came back to get the rest of them. One soldier was a friend of her father's and begged the others to leave the family alone. Pelagie and the rest of the family fled their house to a refugee camp in the southern part of Rwanda and only returned to Gitarama when the war was over.

Pelagie and her sisters were sent to the orphanage, as their mother was unable to care for them alone. She assisted with the younger children at the orphanage and helped the staff hand out clothes and shoes to the children. After the war, when the schools re-opened, she went back to secondary school to finish her studies.

"I am very grateful for how the orphanage helped me to prepare for outside life. They helped me get back to school and integrated me into society. I am excited about the work that the orphanages do and that they help the Government by taking care of so many homeless children."

Pelagie thinks that Rwanda has changed a lot since the war, as people are not so concerned about their backgrounds and family anymore. *"They look at your education more than your background."*

She hopes that orphans can get sponsors or that the Government can help them to study. *"It is very important for all children to have the opportunity to go to school, whatever economical situation they have."*

Pelagie Twagiramariya
Age 24
Region: Nyagacyamu - Ruli, Gitarama.
Working as a nurse in a hospital in Gitarama.
She is married, but has no children.

Jason Nshimyumukiza
Age 23
Region: Kigali.
Attends 1st class in Medical Sciences
at Kigali Health Institute.

"I could not imagine that they would kill little babies..."

Jason grew up in the countryside of Rwanda. When war broke out, he and his family ran to the local church to seek protection. However, the militia soon arrived and attacked, killing most of the people inside. Jason managed to escape with a few other children who hid together in the area for weeks before the Rwandan Patriotic Army found them and relocated them to the Fred Nkunda Life Centre.

Jason's shared his feelings about the war: *"The genocide did not come as a shock to me because there had been many similar wars in Rwanda before. However, I never thought that it would reach the level that it actually did in the end. When the killings started we believed that the militia would only kill the leaders and the educated people. I could not imagine that they would kill little babies and old mothers, which they actually did in large numbers."*

When Jason came to the orphanage he found hope for the future for the first time since the war. The care shown by the staff convinced him that his life could be different, and that he could go back to school and live as a normal kid.

Jason excelled in secondary school and was one of the students whom the Government wanted to sponsor for university. However, instead of continuing his studies he decided to move back to his place of origin. He explains: *"I went home to work as a nurse in the medical clinic to be able to help my mother and two brothers rebuild our house that was destroyed in the war and to help my brother back to school."*

After three years working in Kibuye, Jason is now back in school, this time at Kigali Health Institute where he is studying medical sciences. He wants to become a doctor in order to serve his country by helping sick people. *"Regardless of what happened to me in the past, I have good hopes for my future because I have seen that I will be able to take responsibility for my life. I think that education has become more important because the young people need to take care of themselves. Before the war children were expecting their parents to give them everything, but after the war they have to depend on themselves and therefore want to develop as much as possible."*

Jason found it difficult to understand why the war started: *"I find it very difficult to explain the cause of the genocide. It is impossible for anybody to understand why some people wanted to kill their families, friends and neighbours. I think that one cause of the war might have been ignorance and lack of education."*

He thinks that reconciliation is possible: *"Just eight years after the war students study together and share everything, in spite of what happened between them in the war. I think that in one way it is a miracle that people who have experienced such a great tragedy actually live together like the Rwandan people do today."*

He thinks that Rwanda will become more industrial in the future and that this is positive for the country as it will provide jobs for the people. He suspects that many people will move from the countryside to work in the city. But for him staying in the city is only a matter of being able to support his family and help them to work on the land.

Bringing laughter and joy

Cadeau has lived with his grandparents, Josias and Louise, in the countryside of Kibuye for the last year. He is a happy boy and enjoys playing in the house and fields. He will soon start school and looks forward to learning how to count and read. Most of all, he is excited about making new friends and playing soccer.

The house they live in has no roof. Plastic sheeting is their only protection against strong winds and heavy rainfall. Josias explains: *"When we came back to our place after the war, our house and land were destroyed and we had to start working our land and try to repair the house. We used to be farmers, but because all my children are going to school I had to get a job to pay for their studies."*

At the end of the war Josias and Louise escaped to Congo with their six children. He explains, *"The fighting increased and it was no longer safe for anyone to stay in the country. We went over the border to Congo where we spent three years in refugee camps."*

Their oldest daughter married a man in the refugee camp and Cadeau was born a year later. Then the war broke out in Congo. The family decided to return to Rwanda but were separated from their oldest daughter, her husband and Cadeau .

When the family had arrived safely back in their village they received sad news. *"We were told our daughter was killed while hiding in some bushes between two groups of soldiers who were fighting. When they opened fire she was hit and fell down."*

Cadeau interrupts his grandfather, *"My mother was killed by soldiers. I was with my mother when they shot her. A soldier came to help me and took me to a refugee camp."*

In April 2001 Cadeau came to JAM's Fred Nkunda Life Centre.

The grandfather says, *"We thought that Cadeau had died with his mother until a soldier came to our house with news that our grandson was alive."* The local ICRC office helped them find their grandson.

Josias and Louise are happy to have this little boy in their house. *"We don't know how to express our gratitude for this gift. He brings so much laughter and joy to this house."*

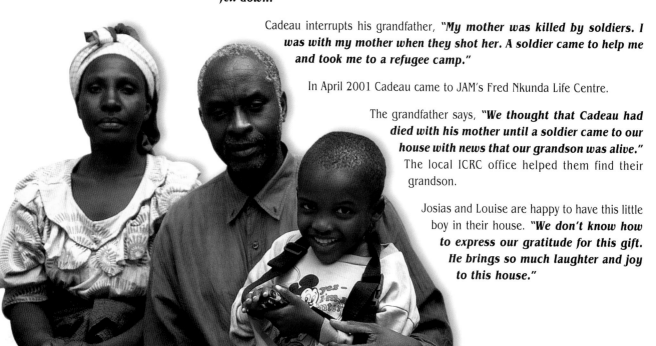

"I thought I would never be able to live a normal life again"

Claire was born in Gisenyi and grew up in a big family. She says: **"I had a very good life before the war started. I was allowed to be a child and did not have to worry about adult matters."**

Militia arrived and burnt down their house and destroyed their livestock – their only means of survival. Claire's family fled to a compound and hid for a period, but soon it was also attacked and she was separated from her parents. Later she found that her father had been murdered and her mother killed in the panic of fleeing.

A missionary came to their rescue and filled his truck with people and took them to a refugee camp in Kabgayi. Here she was reunited with her brothers and sisters. They spent weeks in fear of being separated before they were eventually relocated to an orphanage within the area.

On her first day in the orphanage she felt very lonely and could only think about the loss of her parents: **"The first period after the war was very difficult and I remember that I thought I would never be able to live a normal life again."**

Claire, along with her younger brothers and sisters, spent a long time being relocated from orphanage to orphanage, being separated again and again from one another, until finally they arrived at the Fred Nkunda Life Centre. After settling and experiencing the love of the many housemothers, Claire decided that the JAM Orphanage was the best she had ever stayed in. She explains how loving the mothers and other children are, and how the staff take time to listen to the many troubles they have all experienced.

"They understand our problems" she says, and feels that she has finally found a home.

Claire Mukamuganga
Age 17
Region: Nyarusange village.
Attends S1 at Saint Jean College, Gitarama.

27

Reconciliation through dancing

"I am happy here at the orphanage. What makes me happy is to be able to eat something and to sleep somewhere. I also enjoy going to school, because we discuss things together. I feel happy when I am with other children because it makes me forget what happened in the past. I also like to learn new things and when we as friends get together after school, we discuss our subjects and discuss the work. I like Maths, French and English. For example, if I can speak English, I can one day go to foreigners to ask for a job.

"I would like to continue with my studies and, if I have means, I would like to continue up to university level. I would like to do nursing because it helps to heal people. I can have a good life in future, because I can get a job with a salary. I will then be able to buy food for the house and clothes.

"I like to be with other children, because when you are alone and you try to think, you can sometimes think bad things and you can cry. When you are with other children, you can not only concentrate on bad things. I still sometimes think about the war, especially when I remember my parents. They were farmers and we were happy. I feel sad when I remember how they cared for me.

"I also remember my mother's cooking. Before the war we ate different foods each day, but now we can spend three days eating the same things. At home we used to eat sweet potatoes one day, Irish potatoes the next and then cassava.

"Life will be good if I stay with my brothers and sisters together – not separated everywhere. I miss them, because sometimes I do not know what is happening to them. I wonder many things when I do not get any news from them.

"I also like traditional Rwandan dancing, because I see that people are happy when they see us dancing. I want to bring a dance group of my own together that can then go outside Rwanda to represent the country. When I was dancing in the orphanage, we took first place three times and got three trophies for our efforts. It made me very happy, because our team was good in dancing and when they gave the cups, it was for the whole group. I was really happy to see our team winning. Today, I still dance when there is an event at the orphanage.

Besides dancing, I also wish to continue with studying. If I get a sponsor to study, this will be possible for me. My brother is being helped by 'The Fund for Survivors of the Genocide' to go to secondary school, but I am just waiting and know that God will plan for me."

A British Diplomat from Burundi has agreed to sponsor Clementine right up to university level after seeing her dancing in a celebration at the JAM Fred Nkunda Orphanage.

Clementine Mukamurigo
Age 15
Sister of Claire Mukamuganga

Rescued in a bag

Eugenie currently stays with her two cousins, Bernadette and Emmanuel, in the Bisesero area. They are all under 15 years old and don't have any guardian to look after them. Eugenie explains, ***"When I stayed at the JAM Orphanage I was reunited with my aunt. But I only stayed there for a few weeks before a neighbour asked my aunt if I could come and stay with her to help her in the house. However, I was not treated well and I wanted to leave. A few years later my aunt passed away after being poisoned, and I went back to help my two cousins. Other neighbours wanted to take us to their house but we refused because we did not know them.***

"We survived by digging the land and growing some vegetables. When I go home from school in the holidays I have to work on the land and help in the house. My oldest cousin used to go to school but she had to leave her studies to look after her little brother. We decided that it was best that I continued my studies so that I can help them economically later. We don't have much money at the moment, but some of the neighbours are kind to us and buy school books for me because of our difficult situation.

Eugenie Mukamukomeza
Age 15
Region: Bisesero.
Attends Esapan Secondary School, level 1.

"I seldom think about my future. Most of the time I think about my life as a little girl. Before the war I stayed with my parents and I had everything I could think of. We were so happy and I did not know anything about problems."

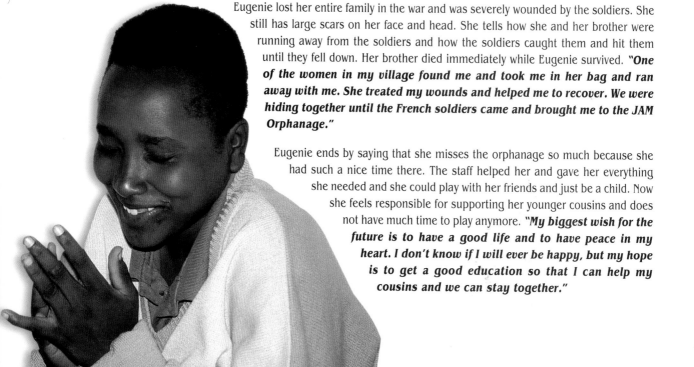

Eugenie lost her entire family in the war and was severely wounded by the soldiers. She still has large scars on her face and head. She tells how she and her brother were running away from the soldiers and how the soldiers caught them and hit them until they fell down. Her brother died immediately while Eugenie survived. ***"One of the women in my village found me and took me in her bag and ran away with me. She treated my wounds and helped me to recover. We were hiding together until the French soldiers came and brought me to the JAM Orphanage."***

Eugenie ends by saying that she misses the orphanage so much because she had such a nice time there. The staff helped her and gave her everything she needed and she could play with her friends and just be a child. Now she feels responsible for supporting her younger cousins and does not have much time to play anymore. ***"My biggest wish for the future is to have a good life and to have peace in my heart. I don't know if I will ever be happy, but my hope is to get a good education so that I can help my cousins and we can stay together."***

"The killers have to face the consequences..."

Vestine's 'mother' and 'father' are now her aunt and uncle with whom she lives in Bisesero, along with her brother and sister. *"I like it here, but I would like to travel and see other places too. I want to go to the city to see what life is like there. One of my biggest dreams is to go outside Rwanda one day. My uncle has told me that it is possible to win a scholarship outside Rwanda if I work hard and succeed in my class. I think it is good to visit other places to learn about different cultures and to become open minded."*

Vestine attends primary school and is doing very well. She wants to become a teacher or a doctor one day, as they earn good money and are capable of looking after themselves.

Even though Vestine was very young when the war started, she remembers many of her war experiences. The militia found them in the bushes because a baby started crying and gave their hiding place away. They slashed her mother many times until she finally died. They also cut her brother's head in two and he died instantly. Some of the soldiers attacked Vestine with sticks and she fell over and acted as though she was dead, like all the others. Once the soldiers thought they had killed everyone, they left the area. Vestine was found a few days later and sent to JAM's Fred Nkunda Life Centre, where her uncle later found her.

"I think that the killers should be punished so that other people will not follow their example. The killers did something horrible and they have to face the consequences of what they did.

"I hope that all Rwandan people will learn to live together and share everything one day. If we can stop the ethnic divisions that have existed in our society, we can have unity among us. The victims from one tribe must try to forget what happened to them in the war and start living in peace with the other tribe."

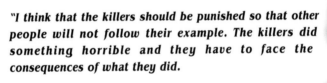

Vestine Mukankundiye
Age 12
Region: Bisesero.
Attends Mumuboga Primary School, level 4.

Hopes for an end to tribalism

Dative is 18 years old and would like to become a nurse to assist people living in the countryside who do not have access to hospitals. Many people in the rural areas do not go to hospital when they are sick, either due to ignorance or because of lack of money. It is also very common in these areas for people to treat themselves with traditional medicine.

"As a nurse I will get the opportunity to help prevent these diseases and teach people simple rules on how to protect themselves. They should also be encouraged to go to the doctor when they are sick and learn how to use medicine correctly."

Dative lives with her brother, his wife and their two small children. They are farmers in Bisesero. Dative told how the soldiers stole their cows to eat them. They also destroyed their house, so they now rent a house in the village nearby so that her brother can work on the farm every day.

Her brother does not have much money but tries to give her all she needs for her studies. When she qualifies she wants to find a job in a hospital, support her brother and help his children attend school.

Dative remembers the days when they were hiding and running from the militia. They ate raw potatoes from the ground when they could find some.

Dative ends her story: *"My biggest wish is that the things that happened in 1994 will never happen again. I hope that the children who grow up will learn to respect each other and that they should not know what tribe they belong to."*

Dative Mukashema
Age 18
Region: Uwingabo, Ngoma.
Attends ESIM Secondary School, level 3.

"You must learn to appreciate what God gives you"

When the war started in Rwanda, Damascine became separated from his family so he went with a group of people across the border into the Democratic Republic of Congo. They stayed in refugee camps until the war spilt over across the border. He was then helped by a man to get back into Rwanda. On arrival, Damascine had no idea where to go. He found some soldiers and they took him to a military camp nearby.

He assisted the soldiers with washing their uniforms, carried their food bags and luggage and he stayed up at night watching for enemies. He was not very happy living with the soldiers, however, so they took him to the JAM Fred Nkunda Life Centre in Gitarama.

Damascine thinks that the war helped him to appreciate life more than ever. The experience has broadened his mind and taught him how to get along with different people. He says, *"When I was in Congo I learnt that life can be very hard at times. Before the war I had never faced any problems and I was very spoilt. During the war I learnt to survive when life was at its most difficult and was still able to think positively. I have learnt that instead of wasting what God gives you, you must learn how to appreciate it. When you have been through some really bad things you become more thankful for the good things God gives you."*

He thinks that one of the reasons for the genocide was greed and says that the people who were involved in the killings were after the other's properties. But he also blames the leaders for the war. *"They created divisions among the people and encouraged them to look at each other as enemies."*

He has forgiven the killers and has put all his memories in the past. He hopes that people will be able to live together in peace like they did before the war.

When asked if he thinks that, as an orphan, he can have a normal life like other children, he says, *"When I leave the orphanage I already know what is good and what is bad, and I will work towards a good life. I think that the orphans will have to work harder to get a good life than other children because when we leave the orphanage we will have to manage on our own while children who have parents will get a lot of support. I think that I will make many mistakes but that I will learn through those mistakes what life is really about and be able to have a normal life at last."*

Jean Damascine Munyeshema
Age 15
Region: JAM Orphanage, Gitarama.
Attends P5 in Shyogwe Primary School.

"*Ignorance causes war*"

Charles is 19 years old and in the middle of his studies at secondary school. He would like to become a teacher when he completes his final exams. *"What my teachers taught me, I want to teach other children. I also find that education is necessary to have a good life and live well. I think that when you study you become open minded and intelligent and you look at things differently than if you have never gone to school.*

"What happened in the war for example was because of ignorance and lack of education. I think that education will help people to develop and again help us to develop our country.

"When you are educated you are able to get a job, which enables you to buy what you need. Uneducated people struggle to survive and they often have to steal, beg or kill to get money."

Charles lost most of his family in the war, but he has a hope of being reunited with his sister. *"IRC has informed me that my sister might be alive and that they are trying to trace her for me. I was born in Kigali and lived with my sister in a village just outside Kigali. When the war got worse, my sister, her husband and I decided to leave our house.*

Charles Ngirinshuti
Age 19
Region: JAM Orphanage, Gitarama.
Attends Apeserwa Secondary School in Gisenyi, level 3.

"We met a group of soldiers who wanted to kill us, but luckily one of them knew my sister and her husband very well. He told the other soldiers that he would take care of us and then brought us out of the village. He told us to run away and not return to the village before the war was over."

Charles and his sister decided that it was best to separate. He ran to Kigali where he met some of his neighbours and they offered to help him hide in a Catholic church with them. He explains that the Saint Paul Cathedral in Kigali was one of the few churches that were protected by UN soldiers during the war. *"Sometimes groups of militia came to attack and wanted to get in, but the UN soldiers fought to stop them and no one was killed inside the church."*

After the war Charles was relocated to the JAM Fred Nkunda Life Centre where he still stays. *"When I came to JAM I had a warm welcome and I was allowed to continue my studies."*

Charles thinks that the war must have started as a result of *"greediness of power and lack of education."* He shared with us the feeling that the people who started the war were those who wanted ALL the power to themselves. The leaders of these groups taught their people to kill others in order to continue to have the power.

"A good future for Rwanda will be a country without any division and with good leadership."

"The war took all my dearest ones away"

Alphonse came from a very poor family. He says: *"Before the war my parents had no cows and only a small piece of land to work. I was one of nine children so it was difficult for my parents to get food for all of us."*

When the war started the family all separated hoping that at least some of them would survive. However, Alphonse was the only one. *"The war took all my dearest ones away. I remember that just before the war ended, big groups of militia came to Kibuye where I live and they killed many people. The ones who survived were those who managed to hide in bushes until the RP soldiers came to help us.*

"I was relocated to the Fred Nkunda Life Centre where I lived for a couple of years before I was reunited with my cousin. I was happy to go with him because I believed that he would help me with all my needs both in school and at home.

"However, when I came to his house, life became difficult. I had to drop out of school because my cousin wanted me to look after his cows and work on his land. I was digging the land from early morning to late evening. He did not give me any clothes and I did not get enough food every day. If he only could have offered to help me with my needs I would have no problems helping him on his farm but he never did."

After some years his uncle realised how bad the situation was and invited Alphonse to stay with him. *"He is an old man and very poor, but he works hard to help me with my school materials and whatever else I need. I am happy to stay with someone who treats me well, even though all my physical needs are not always met.*

"My biggest wish is to succeed in my education and get the means to help my country by giving things to people who do not have anything. A very important part of rebuilding Rwanda is for people to start helping each other."

Alphonse Ngiriyeze
Age 18
Region: Julwe/Bisesero.
Attends Esapan Secondary School, level 2.

Charlotte Ngiruwonsanga
Age 17
Region: Rubengera Orphanage, Kibuye.
Attends Rubengera Primary School, level 6.

Saved by a kind lady

Charlotte stays together with her two younger sisters in Rubengera Orphanage in Kibuye. She is completing her final year at primary school and is very excited about starting secondary school. *"I want to study to become a nurse because I want to help sick people. When people are seriously sick today they have to wait too long to get treatment when they come to the hospital. I want to be an efficient nurse who helps people immediately when they get sick."*

The girls quickly settled at the orphanage and are happy. *"We like this orphanage because we stay in families and we have everything we need here. We have to help to prepare food and clean the house, which is very useful. I am happy about that even though it is quite boring sometimes.*

"When we leave the orphanage we want to live together in our own house. We will save money to build a house when we have finished our education. My biggest dream is to go back to our place of origin. After the war some neighbours who had survived the war came to visit me. They told me that they were looking after my land and invited me to come and look at it. They then suggested that I should rent the land to people so that I could save some money for my sisters and me.

"When we were living in Kibuye Orphanage we had to spend the money on school materials, but since we came to this orphanage I have been able to put aside some money because they give us all we need. I want to save enough money to buy a cow for us so that we can start fertilising the land. I would like to grow beans, maize, cabbage, carrots and other different vegetables. I want to use the vegetables in our own meals but if we get good harvests I want to give food to the poor people in the village.

"When the war broke out I did not understand what was going on myself, I just saw many people from my village being killed and my parents told us that we had to leave our house. We were running towards the stadium in Kibuye when we met a group of militia. They stopped my mother and chopped her to death with a panga."

The soldiers did not harm the young girls when they found them and took them to a woman they knew where they stayed until the war was over. *"The lady was very nice to me and she protected me from the killers. She was married to a man from the opposite tribe who was hiding close to her house. One day someone told her that he had been killed and she took me with her and ran towards Goma because she was scared of being killed herself. When the war was over we went back to Kibuye. The lady took me to the French soldiers who relocated me to the Fred Nkunda Life Centre in Gitarama."*

Top of the class

Valois lost his parents in the genocide. His sisters, who were taking care of him, had already been in secondary school for two years and had no option but to bring him to the JAM Fred Nkunda Life Centre to be taken care of.

He is happy to stay at the orphanage because the staff send him to school, but looks forward to moving back to his sisters one day because he misses them much and loves them dearly. *"I am waiting for them to finish secondary school and come fetch me from the orphanage so that we can live together again.*

"Before the war I was staying with my sisters and my parents in Kigali. I don't remember anything from the war, but my sisters have told me that when it started my mother placed me on her back and ran away with my father. My parents were killed but my sisters found me where the dead bodies were and took me home."

When asked if he likes to go to school, he says: *"I like to study because I am the best in my class. The last test I did, I had 183 out of 200, which is very good. I don't have any favourite subjects because I do well in all of them."*

Valois wants to become a teacher as he thinks it is important to help the children in finishing their studies and in obtaining a decent education. *"It is good for the children to attend school so that they can avoid becoming street boys. I know many street boys from Kigali. They don't have any place to sleep or anything to eat. They have to beg from people to survive.*

"I will teach the children the importance of becoming independent and self producing. If the children who grow up can learn how to make things by themselves they will be able to develop themselves and the country as well.

"I think that the people who committed the genocide are very bad people. However, I have forgiven the ones who killed my mother, but if they start another war they have gone too far and they don't deserve to be forgiven.

"A good life is to live in peace and have a good relationship with the people around you. When I watch television I see that hatred still exists between people and that there are wars going on all over the world.

"People must encourage other people, instead of talking bad about them."

Valois Rugamba
Age 9-11
Region: JAM Orphanage, Gitarama.
Attends Shyogwe Primary School, level 3.

Still looking for her mother

Adela stays at the JAM Fred Nkunda Life Centre at the moment and is very happy. ***"The staff take good care of me. I am very thankful for what the orphanages do for the children who lost their parents in the war. They take care of us while they look for our relatives. I think that most children would be better off living in a family because there they learn how to relate to each other.***

"I would LOVE to find my mother. My father died in the war, but my mother might still be alive. IRC has been looking for my mother since I came back to Rwanda and I hope that they will manage to find her one day."

Adela grew up in Gisenyi, which is close to the border between Rwanda and the Democratic Republic of Congo. In 1990, the Rwandan Patriotic Army was forced out of the country and tried to come back into Rwanda through Gisenyi. The Government soldiers stopped them on the border and so the fighting began.

"I remember that we were close to Kivu Lake when we heard gunfire around us. My mother ran away but my father got scared, fell in the lake and drowned. I fell as well but one of the soldiers took my arm and helped me to my feet. I refused to go with him and ran in the direction that my mother had run."

She tried to find her mother but had no luck. She met up with a Congolese girl who took her over the border to her own family. Adela stayed with this family for a few years before IRC found her and relocated her to an orphanage in Rwanda.

Adela has hopes for the future and she thinks that reconciliation is possible. ***"The society has changed because the leaders are teaching us to love each other and they condemn what happened in the war. I think that reconciliation will be possible because most of the people who were involved in the genocide have realised that what they did was a terrible act and have asked for forgiveness. I think that if people will follow what the leaders teach us, we will have peace in the future.***

"I would like to help my country to develop, by sharing with others what happened in the genocide. I think that if we tell others about the war we can prevent it from happening again."

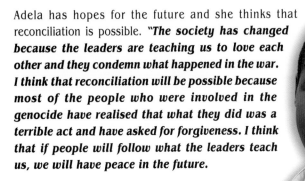

Adela Umutesi
Age 14
Region: JAM Orphanage, Gitarama.
Attends Mbare Primary School, level 4.

Marie Jeanne Usabyimbabazi
Age 15
Region: Murangara, Kibuye.
Attends ESIM Secondary School, level I.

Still feels pain thinking about the war

Marie Jeanne stays with her aunt and uncle on their land in the countryside of Kibuye. She is happy as they treat her well and have a good relationship with each other. Marie assists her aunt with the cooking and cleaning of the house when she comes home for her school holidays and enjoys learning how to take care of the home. This has prepared her for her own home one day when she is married.

Marie Jeanne stayed in JAM's Fred Nkunda Life Centre for quite some time until Save the Children traced her aunt and uncle in Kibuye and reunited them. They were happy to have Marie Jeanne come and live with them and she was very excited to go back to the countryside where she was born and be a part of a real family again for the first time since the war.

She says: **"When the war broke out in my area, I ran with my family to the local church. We were about 6000 people, squeezed into the building. I think the reason for all of us coming to the church was that we did not believe that anybody would dare to kill us while we were inside the house of God. However, a group of militia came and opened fire on us. After shooting they used traditional arms to kill the ones who were still alive. Most of the people were killed. Only a few strong boys and children managed to run away. All the people standing close to me fell down and died. I was not hit because I was so little, but I fell down and lay still until the militia was gone.**

"The only one I could think of was my aunt who stayed close to our house and I ran to see if she was at home. She was married to a man from the opposite tribe and he had not been killed yet. They were home and decided to hide me in the house. I stayed with them until the end of the war. The French soldiers came and felt it was not safe for me to stay there so they brought me to a refugee camp in Bisesero. The killings continued and it was still not safe in the area. A few days later we were relocated to Gitarama where we went to the JAM Orphanage.

"I often think about the war but it is very painful to know that I am the only one who survived in my family. I hope that one day I will be able to think about the war without feeling pain. I will try to forget about it by keeping myself busy doing other things."

Learning a skill

Claudine arrived at the Fred Nkunda Life Centre two years ago. When the war broke out in her village in 1994, her mother was killed immediately, but she managed to escape with her father and brother. However a few days later they were all separated and she followed strangers, not knowing where to go. She ended up in a refugee camp in Congo and was relocated to an orphanage. The war grew worse near the orphanage so she managed to escape and run away. She was lucky enough to meet one of the orphanage supervisors whilst on the run, who felt sorry for Claudine and took her home with her.

When the war was over and it was safe to return to Rwanda, a relief organisation relocated Claudine to the JAM Orphanage in Gitarama. Here she attends sewing classes at the new training centre and is happy to learn a technical skill that will assist her in becoming a tailor one day. *"I have enjoyed sewing since I was a little girl, but the training Centre was my first opportunity to learn it as a skill. I like the training centre because children who have the same interests come together and can get to know each other."*

Claudine is very thankful to the orphanage for what they have taught her, but is concerned about the future of the other orphans. *"I am happy to be in the orphanage, but orphans face problems that other children never ever think of. I think that orphans have to struggle and work harder than other children to get a good life because they have no one to help them and advise them. The orphans have to discover themselves how to get a job and how to get a good life. I find it difficult to be without a family and not knowing what the future will bring.*

"I hope that I will have a good life in the future. My friends and I often talk about how the future will be and we encourage each other by saying that God will take care of us.

"For me, a good life is to live in peace and to have good relationships with the people around you. A good life is a life without any war."

She sees positive development in her country and she thinks that Rwanda will become a good place to live in, in the future. *"Today there is a great change going on in Rwanda. During the war, people did not share anything with each other but now people live and work together without any problem and they relate to each other as friends."*

Claudine Uwamaliya

Age 17
Region: JAM Orphanage, Gitarama.
Attends sewing classes in the new training centre in the orphanage.

"I believe in the power of prayer"

Born in Mwendo, Kibuye, in 1982, Anne Marie came to the JAM Orphanage in December 1994 at the age of 12. Sharing her life with other children who came from similar experiences has helped her to avoid the extreme loneliness of someone who has lost their entire family.

Anne Marie becomes quiet and distracted when reminded of the genocide. It is still too difficult for her to recall.

After completing a course in tailoring, this shy, soft-spoken girl started working as a seamstress at the orphanage, mending the tatters that the orphans wear, often re-designing them into respectable creations.

With a smile, she asserts that if she had the means, she would start a tailoring workshop where women can come and learn from her.

"Life is very expensive in Rwanda but I believe that my dream will come true one day. I also recommend other children to attend the course in tailoring at the orphanage because of what my skill has meant to me. Training like this can help them when they leave the security of the orphanage to work outside."

Anne Marie wants to get married and have children one day but she still does not feel that peace is something she can believe yet. She says: *"The war might be over in Rwanda, but it still rages on in other countries. If a war ends in a place, it is just a matter of time before it starts again. I am afraid of this.*

" I am a firm believer in God and can say with sincerity that I believe in the power of prayer and that it can change my country. I accepted Christ three years after the war, learning about Jesus for the first time while at the orphanage. He means everything to me now. I wish that people would live together in peace and harmony."

Anne Marie lives one kilometre from the JAM Orphanage with another ex-JAM orphan called Donatha, who is working at JAM as a cook.

Anne Marie Mukamugenga
Age 20
Region: Shyogwe in the Gitarama Prefecture.
Employed by JAM as a Seamstress.

"*I don't know if God has forgiven them...*"

Bosco came to the JAM Orphanage in October 2000 and was happy to do so because he knew that the orphanage could help him find his relatives.

He recalls how they left his grandmother and grandfather behind in Gikongoro when he fled with his parents. He would like to find them if they are still alive. Tracing agencies have been unable to locate them. Bosco says that his biggest wish is to get his parents back.

He does not remember much of the genocide, except people being **"cut and killed with pangas"**.

Bosco tells how he was living peacefully with his family. They needed to flee to Congo when the genocide started. En route, they were apprehended by armed people in a vehicle and commanded to sit down. His father was carrying a small radio. The men took the radio and beat his father over the head until he died. They then tortured his mother, making her lie down in front of their vehicle and driving over her. Seeing this, Bosco escaped into the dense forest where he joined a group of refugees. They drank dirty water and ate roots and leaves to survive and finally arrived in the Congo.

While in the forest, a primate dropped a branch from a tree. This broke the femur of his right leg. A Congolese man who happened to pass by heard him groaning, had pity on him and took him to his house. Bosco's leg healed naturally, but the bone mended in the wrong position.

He tries to exercise his leg and believes that it will get better. Bosco is now able to hop and run short distances on his leg without supporting it with his hands.

Bosco was too young at the time of the genocide to remember his relatives or what Rwanda was like before the genocide but he resents the killers, saying: **"They have done a very bad thing to me. They made me an orphan and I am now deformed. I have forgiven them, but I don't know if God has forgiven them."**

Bosco Hafashimana
Age 13
Born in Kabari, Gikongoro.
Region: JAM Orphanage, Gitarama.

"*Teach the bad people to follow the good way*"

During the war Toto's family fled, with others, to Saki in the Democratic Republic of Congo. People shot at them and everyone ran in different directions. He became separated from his parents in 1994.

"*I am in an orphanage now. If my situation was good, I would not be here, but I have nowhere to go. If I get a family or if I find my parents I feel that I need to go back to my place of origin. I could have been in our lands, starting to till the ground and to be a farmer.*

"*I think my parents are still alive. One day, I went to our area with an NGO who does tracing of relatives and I saw that my parents weren't there. When we reached Gisenyi, we sent a message to my place and we were told that there was nobody there and then we came back. At that moment I didn't feel sad because if I stay in one place, like the orphanage, and they still broadcast our names over the radio, my parents will get the message that I am still alive and then come to find me.*

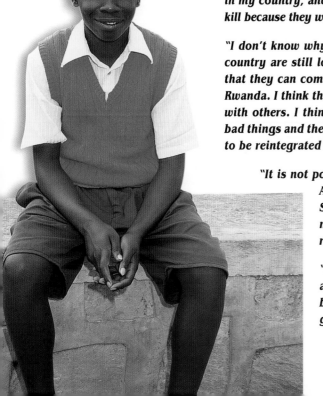

Toto Hakizimana
Age 17
Born in Gisenyi Town in Gisenyi Province.
Region: JAM Orphanage, Gitarama.
Attends P3 in Mbare Primary School.

"*I spent seven years in the DRC. The men had problems there, because when the people saw that they were staying with Congolese families, the Interahamwe Militia came and took them to be trained as soldiers. As children, we were living with Congolese families without a problem. I wasn't happy, because I was not in my country, and besides, the Congolese were starting to look for Rwandans to kill because they were saying that they did not want Rwandan people there.*

"*I don't know why the genocide happened in Rwanda. The people outside the country are still looking for people to join them to increase their numbers so that they can come back to Rwanda to fight. I don't know why they don't like Rwanda. I think that they are bad people, because they don't like to be in peace with others. I think these people should be punished, because they did many bad things and they were wrong. I would like it if they will come back peacefully to be reintegrated into the Rwandan Army.*

"*It is not possible now, but I see that it will be possible if the Rwandan Army went in a big number to search for them to disarm them. Some people in Congo still destroy everything. Even if you meet them in the road, they ask you for money and, if you refuse, they can come and kill you in the night.*

"*I wish that the things that happened in 1994 will not happen again. Many people suffered in the war. My opinion is that the bad people can go to a seminar to be taught to follow the good way...*"

Plans to help other orphans

Gerard's father, uncles, grandfathers and grandmothers all died in the war, and his mother died just one month after the war ended, because of the injuries and problems she suffered as a result of the fighting. Gerard's oldest brother takes care of him now, as head of the family.

Gerard says: **"I like school and have already applied for electronics, because many people have told me about the benefits of this field. I plan to work for myself, e.g. fixing radios and televisions.**

"We had to move from Butare, where my father was a doctor, because my family's property was stolen and destroyed and we had to start over.

"When I think of these things today it does not make me very sad, because I try to forget it. I think I can have a normal life when I have finished my studies and will try to help myself."

Gerard Bizimana
Age 18
Born in Mngasa, Butare.
Attends Shyogwe Secondary School.

Gerard's brother (27) had one year left to finish primary school teacher training before the war, but he had to stop studying to take care of the family. He is married, and has a child, and helps all seven brothers and sisters.

Gerard is doing well at school. **"I got 68 percent average in my class. I am in tenth position out of 40 children, because I work hard.**

"When I am finished, and find means, I can take some orphans home and help them. I plan to do this when I complete my studies. I want to do this because I am an orphan myself and for me it is so hard to manage life. I also feel sorry for other orphans. If my parents had been alive, I would have studied to become a doctor like my father, but it will not be possible for me. My father even used to help people go outside the country to study. As my father's own child, I could have expected that he would also have paid for me to send me outside the country to study.

"I can try and help them in place of their parents that they have lost. I can try to show them sufficient love and give them anything they particularly need. When my parents were still alive, I felt that they would have done anything for me to study and also to reach a high level of achievement. I will do the same for the children that I will help.

"I wish that every person from a young age will take a decision for his future and decide what important things he can do for himself and, by that decision, help those weaker than him who cannot reach the same level. People should be encouraged to make decisions that can fulfil them and enable them to help others.

"I would even like this for the sake of my country. Whenever anybody asks for forgiveness and accepts the mistake he made, of course he needs to be forgiven. Unfortunately, not everybody regrets what he or she did. Even if it is because of other people that I am where I am, it is up to me to carry on with my life."

Brothers reunited

Pascal and Justin are two brothers who were amongst seven children of their family that survived the genocide. Pascal is currently employed at the JAM Fred Nkunda Orphanage where he works as a cook. His brother Justin attends school nearby and lives at the orphanage. Pascal is married to Rosine Uuimana. Together they have a little daughter, Pascaline.

Like many people, they lived happily with their parents, tending the cattle and working the land as their family had done so many times before. Chaos erupted when militia attacked their village. Their entire family had to race in all directions, taking refuge in the forest, the local church and hospital.

Pascal was separated from his parents while fleeing to the mountains. Justin was told to run when the militia murdered his father. He knew that this was the beginning of a terrible, lonely life and many of his family were never seen again.

While in the mountains, the young boys had to take cover during the day in fear of being discovered, and only emerged at night to learn about who may or may not have survived the terrible attack, and to find the injured and offer help wherever they could. Pascal says: **"The militia found me and my two brothers hiding in a ditch. Granite slabs were thrown on us and I injured my leg. I escaped, and watched from a distance how my younger brother was tied to a tree and beaten to death with sticks."**

Justin Nzabahimana
Age 17
Born in Kibuye,
Region: JAM Orphanage, Gitarama.
Attending Shyogwe Primary School, level 5.

Finally the war was over and, yet again, Pascal and Justin were separated as they were taken to different refugee camps to have wounds medically treated. It was during this time that the boys heard about the JAM International life-saving haven orphanage.

Both were taken in and given love and help. Later in the year, Pascal was offered full time employment and Justin was offered a chance to be educated. Their, dream is, however, to be able to return to their home town and begin a new life on the land they once called home. Until then, they remain a part of the daily life at the JAM Fred Nkunda Life Centre, giving hope to many of those children who went through different atrocities with the same devastating results of a war they will never understand.

Pascal Hategekimana
Age 26
Region: Shyogwe village, Gitarama.
Employed by JAM as a cook since September 1994.

A Business Man

Ismael fled to Uganda with his parents in 1990 when the uprising started in Rwanda, but was separated from his parents at the border. He was six at the time.

"In Uganda I stayed with soldiers in a military camp, doing chores like carrying water," Ismael says. *"The camp was attacked in 1992 and expatriate Rwandan families tried to persuade the children to live with them and help in their homes. I did so, and this family helped me to attend school."*

The family had a small business and the father taught Ismael some business skills, which he intends to capitalise on when he leaves the orphanage in the near future.

"In 2000, when I was 16 and when the war finally seemed to be over in my home country, I decided to search for my parents. The family I was staying with gave me the taxi fare to Tanzania to look for my parents among the other Rwandan refugees."

Ismael was placed in an orphanage while his name was put on a list and was broadcast in the refugee camps. During this time he started a small business selling biscuits in the refugee camp. He found nobody who knew him and after a month returned to Rwanda.

The UNHCR (United Nations High Commission for Refugees) helped Ismael and transferred him to JAM's Fred Nkunda Life Centre. He was placed on a programme run by the IRC to helps adolescent orphans reintegrate into society by providing houses for them.

He is now looking forward to carrying on with his life – moving into his own place, starting a small business, selling basic items like bread in the same way that the family did where he stayed Uganda.

Ismael still thinks of his past, but says that he would rather forget those things. He notices a change in the people of Rwanda. They respect and love one another more than before. *"When I think about what happened, I feel that something as bad as this can't happen again, because Rwandans learnt from the war. Parents lost their children, some lost husbands or wives so many lives were destroyed, therefore the people won't allow this to happen again.*

"I believe people want to go back to what they did before: to buy cows and start afresh, but they have very little money or means to build their farms again. My highest wish is to see peace in my country and people living together without hatred and fighting."

Ismael says that when he listens to the radio, he can tell that a new generation of people is living in Rwanda today.

Ismael Tuyizere
Age 18
Born in Kagitumba.
Region: JAM Orphanage, Gitarama since 2000.

"I thought I didn't have anybody left"

"When the war started in our area, my mother decided she could not suffer without her family... We left our father and went to my mother's area. The situation there was very bad. We were two brothers, one sister and my baby brother who went with my mother. One day, the killers found my mother and we heard how they were cutting her with machetes. We also heard how they started to cut my baby brother and my sister. At the moment that my brother and I heard our sister and the baby being cut, we decided that if we cried out and ran, that they would follow us and stop cutting them. We cried out and ran, but the killers didn't follow us.

"When we came back, we saw that our mother and our sister had died, but the baby was still breathing although his condition was very bad. We took him with us, but after a few minutes he also died. After this, my brother and I decided to separate and not to hide together.

"One day I heard a lot of shooting and saw that everybody was running away. It was a chance to run in the safety of a big group. I was so young that no one asked me who I was."

Jean de Dieu Kubwimana
Age 16
Born in Ngoma, Butare.
Region: JAM Orphanage, Gitarama.
Attends P4 in Shyogwe Primary School.

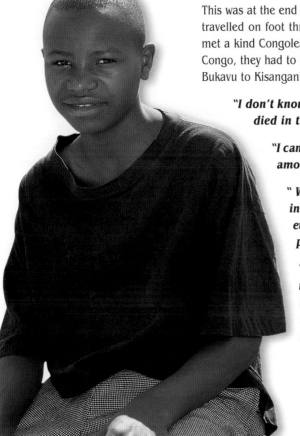

This was at the end of the war when people were running from Rwanda to Congo. Jean travelled on foot through Butare to Gikongoro, Cyangugu and Bukavu. In Bukavu he met a kind Congolese man who took him to live in his house. When the war started in Congo, they had to run away and Jean was separated from the man. He travelled from Bukavu to Kisangani, then to Kigali with some refugees.

"I don't know how my father died, but I received information that he had died in the war. Now both my parents were dead.

"I came to the orphanage and was so happy to find my older brother among the other children. I thought I didn't have anybody left.

" When I am playing, I start to forget the things that happened in the war, but during the annual week of mourning, I remember everything. This week is not good for me, because I get many problems when I remember and I feel sad.

"One thing I like to do now is study because I see that this will help me in the future. I have not started to think about my future after my studies, but I would like to do something that will help me to forget the things that have happened to me."

Jean Paul Iyamuremye
Age 14
Finished with P4 in primary school.
Region: JAM Orphanage, Gitarama.

"People can be reconciled through understanding"

Jean Paul is HIV positive. He is aware of his illness and does not like it because of the way that some children treat him when they see the sores. He stopped going to school because he is often sick. He attends art and drawing class at the orphanage training centre because he feels that it will help him in the future. He would like to do signwriting for a living. His healthy younger brother, Jean Pierre, sits next to him in drawing class in the holidays.

He describes himself in a deeply philosophical way: *"For my life... I like peace, love, to keep quiet, and to be peaceful with my friends."* He would like to learn to speak English properly and says that he likes meeting people from foreign countries.

He cannot remember much of the war. *"I was very young, maybe five years old. In the day I was not afraid, but I was at night. I stayed with my parents in Kigali. UN soldiers always protected the area. We listened on the radio to hear what was happening on the newscasts."*

One day soldiers came and took his father away. *"My mother, my brother and I were taken to a school in Kigali where we stayed until the war ended. One day I heard people talking that my father had a broken leg, but we never saw or heard of him again. I hope that he is still alive and that he will return one day."*

His mother became very ill and died. Their relatives could not care for them so they came to the JAM Orphanage.

"People can be reconciled with one another by learning to understand each other and by asking forgiveness for what happened. Then there will be peace.

"It is possible that my illness can be treated and healed one day, if I can get the right medicine. I will have a good life and do what I am learning in the drawing class. I plan to live a full life and would like to go further with the talent of drawing that God has given me."

Louise Mukagatare
Age 17
Born in Butare.
Attends college at St. Jean, Nyaryusange.

"It is good to study"

Louise loves studying and dislikes any form of laziness so she hates to miss school. She had to stay away from school for a whole year because of problems with the paper work that orphans have to produce every year to qualify for bursaries. She is at her happiest when she is at school.

"It is good to study, because you study and learn what you did not know before. If I do well in my studies, it can help me to find a good job one day.

"There are more girls today that are studying than before the war. The government changed. Before, there were'nt many girls who were going to school, but today anybody who would like to study has a chance to go.

"I would like to have a husband and children one day, but that will come later on. First of all, I need to study. When I have children, they will stay at home while I am at work. I will be able to hire someone to look after the children because I will be educated and will have a job. This depends on the quality of life I will have. My children should not go without clothes or milk to drink while I am working, but I need to work for them and get means for their futures.

"My brother is in P5 in Shyogwe Primary and in some way I feel responsible for him. His name is James and he is 15 years old. As his senior, I feel as if I need to convince him to love studying and to encourage him. I like to be responsible, because I am the one who has to look after him, especially to encourage him to study so that we will have a good life one day."

Louise says that she and her brother don't talk about the genocide that occurred in Rwanda in 1994, because: *"we all know what happened to us and there is no reason to talk to each other and repeat it."*

The events that happened in Rwanda have changed the future for Louise. She has been made an orphan as a result of the genocide and has been robbed of her family and parents. However, she also feels that the genocide taught people not to follow blindly what the authorities teach them.

"People think for themselves now and understand the authorities and there is a balance today between the good and the bad."

Beatrice Mukamwiza
Age 24
Housewife with two children staying in
Kagitarama with her husband.

Finding happiness through marriage

Beatrice is happily married and lives with her husband, Augustine, and their two children. They came from the same area and faced similar difficulties through the war. They have been married for seven years. Augustine worked with an Italian company that repaired the roads after the war, but when the company pulled out of the country all the employees had to look for other jobs.

"We just try to grow some food on the land we rent, enough to survive. Things are difficult for us, because the war brought us here.

"When the war broke out, the people on the hills tried to protect themselves by throwing stones, but the attackers had guns and we could not keep fighting against them. Everybody had an equal chance of surviving or being killed. Sometimes the killers came at night and threw grenades at groups who were sleeping. My whole family died in the genocide.

"They beat me with a heavy stick on the head. I only survived because I just lay still where I fell among the bodies. I tried to smear myself with blood to pretend that I was dead. I waited for the night to try and move from there to join other people. I still get headaches from my injury.

"People tried to help hide those with bad injuries, and those who couldn't walk, in the bushes. In the evenings they would come and find you and treat your wounds and hide you from the killers again. My cousin helped me.

"When the French started to maintain security in the area, they urged us to come under their protection and stop hiding. We still felt as if we were going to die. We did not know that someone would come to save us. In one of the compounds in Kabgayi, I started feeling safe and started thinking properly.

"We later heard that near the compound there was an organisation that was taking care of orphans. I was 15 years old when they told me that I could stay at the JAM Fred Nkunda Orphanage. I went back to school, but was always thinking about what happened and I was also suffering from headaches because of my injury. Especially when I was sleeping, I kept remembering how one of my younger brother's head was split in two by a panga.

"I was in the orphanage for about a year when I went to live with my cousin in Gitarama. I met my husband there. We knew each other from before the war. I was happy to marry someone who knew my life and also someone whose life I knew. Married life makes me happy. It will also make me happy to be able to send my five-year-old boy and three-year-old girl to school when they grow up. The girl's name is Solange and the boy's name is Aimable.

"Up to now, we have had enough energy to look for food. We try our best to grow sweet potatoes. At least the house we live in is ours..."

Horror upon horror

Solange was a mere seven years old when she witnessed the most horrific atrocities. Her life, like many others, was to change forever – a life of fear, never forgetting what she had seen.

Solange and her family were fortunate to live in a home that was surrounded by a high wall. Over that wall, they were able to hear much shouting and killing going on. Solange's mother had promised her husband that she would never leave him, so she sent Solange to stay with a friend. Some days later, Solange returned home to find her mother and brothers outside, talking to some soldiers whilst her father was still inside the house. Solange's mother was related to the soldiers and, although she had never seen them before, believed that they were her uncles. Her father was told he was to take his two sons and follow the soldiers. Solange's mother refused, and said that the only thing that could separate them as a family would be death.

Solange watched from her bedroom window as the soldiers lined up her entire family and opened fire. She saw each of her family members fall to the ground. Their clothes were removed, as well as any other items they had on their bodies. Days went by as a terrified Solange hid in her bedroom and watched as neighbours and strangers alike walked into their home and looted all they could carry.

Finally a lady came in and gathered some cloth to cover the bodies of the once close Mukeshimana family. Solange felt she could trust this lady and left home with her. After two days of living in the home of this stranger, soldiers arrived with a pig. They cooked the animal and insisted the lady eat. She refused and so they shot her dead.

Solange fled and took refuge with an elderly lady at her home. However, when they heard gunshots a few days later, they decided to run and seek refuge in another village. On the way, they were confronted by soldiers and asked where the lady had found Solange. The soldiers wanted to know about the belongings in Solange's home and accused her rescuer of stealing them. After denying this accusation the soldiers opened fire on the lady and killed her.

We don't know why Solange's life was spared, but the soldiers took her with them to their camp and later moved her to the town of Butare where she stayed until the end of the war.

Authorities finally placed Solange in the JAM Fred Nkunda Orphanage. In 1997 she was moved to an orphanage nearer to her home as it would be easier to locate any living relatives. An uncle finally located Solange, hired a nursemaid and placed them together in a house he had bought. He worked for the military and was often away and, on his death in 1998, Solange was removed from the care of the nursemaid and sent back to the JAM Orphanage where she now stays and is happy.

"I would like to be a nurse some day. It is something that is simple for me and it is also a humanitarian action. I like the concept of helping people, as I am also helped by people."

Solange Mukeshimana
Age 15
Region: JAM Orphanage, Gitarama.
Attends Bare Primary School P4.

Abandoned – but not by JAM

Lea came to the orphanage in 1997. She was abandoned by her mother in the hospital, shortly after she was born. Lea's mother asked a lady to look after her child while she went for a walk, but never returned. The lady approached the local authorities explaining what had happened. She was given a letter and asked to take the child to the JAM Fred Nkunda Orphanage. Lea was only a few months old when she first arrived and has never again been visited by the lady who originally took her there.

Lea is now seven years of age and is totally deaf and dumb. She has a wonderful nature and is well liked by all. She loves to play with the other children and is always considering others before herself. The only manner in which Lea knows how to communicate is by sign language, which is often frustrating for her to get her feelings across to people. When people speak very slowly (in her mother tongue) she is able to lip-read. The JAM house mothers have recognised Lea's attentiveness and eagerness to learn and they have taught her as much as they know. The specialised training Lea needs to enhance her current abilities is very expensive and the best JAM can offer her now is to train her in pottery or sewing at the JAM Training Centre.

JAM's vision for these children is to be able to reunite them with their families or place them into good foster homes. A lot of research and work goes into looking for blood parents or foster parents and JAM works very closely with the Rwandan Government in making sure that the right decisions are made in the child's best interest. Many prospective parents look for children who are very young, whom they can raise in a particular way without clashes or difficulties. So the older the children get, the harder it is to find them a family. Nevertheless, JAM will always do their best to find each orphan the best family possible, where they can each have a life worth living.

Lea Muragitjimana
Age 7
Born in Mushibata village.
Region: JAM Orphanage, Gitarama.
Attends pre-school at the orphanage.

JAM helps Florentine stitch her life back together

Having lost her father to disease some years before the war, Florentine's mother, two younger sisters and brother were left to fend for themselves when the soldiers started their reign of terror in the nearby area. "*My two younger sisters and I managed to escape as the soldiers dragged my mother and brother down to the Nyaborongo River. My brother drowned almost instantly and my mother was thrown into the river again and again after trying to escape the deep waters, until she, too, finally succumbed and died.*"

After several weeks of hiding, Florentine heard that her two sisters had survived and had been taken in by two families offering them refuge. At that time Florentine was living with an elderly lady who ended up treating her as a slave, demanding that she work as her housemaid. "*I managed to run away and was placed in the JAM Fred Nkunda Orphanage by the local authorities after I pleaded with them for help. This was in January 2001.*"

Florentine Nikuze

Age 18
Born in Gitarama, Rwanda.
Region: JAM Orphanage, Gitarama.
Finished primary school Level 4 in 2001, now attending sewing class in the new training centre.

Since her arrival at the home of hundreds like herself, Florentine has had to drop out of school due to severe eye problems. She has been learning to sew in the JAM Training Centre and, because she is now 18 years of age, JAM would like to see her successfully integrated back into society, a prospect she finds very exciting. She would love to go back to school to complete her studies, as she loves to learn, but until she can get the correct treatment for her eye condition, she will continue to sew. She plans to work as a seamstress or a shopkeeper to earn enough money to take care of her two sisters and move into their own little home. JAM continues to love and protect her, and will not force her to leave until she is absolutely ready to cope with society again, irrespective of her age.

Donatha Morekeyisoni
Age 23
Born in Kibuye.
Region: Shyogwe village, near JAM Orphanage, Gitarama.
Employed by JAM as a cook since 1997.

Donatha finds the recipe for happiness

Donatha is a young lady who appears shy and nervous when asked about her experiences during the genocide. Like most of the children, this was a traumatic time and is very difficult to talk about. During a relaxed conversation with her, she told us **"I like to work, pray and read my Bible. I also dream of becoming a nurse."**

Later she tearfully began to tell her story about her awful memories: **"No one has ever explained to me why the genocide took place. It seems everyone just keeps quiet as they are too afraid to talk about the past. They just want to forget."**

Donatha and her family fled their home on 12 April 1994 after militia attacked their village and murdered her father. She and a few family members took refuge in a local church, but two days later militia attacked once again, destroying the building by driving heavy machinery into it, killing all but Donatha. Convinced that every last person was dead, the militia left, giving Donatha a chance to run for her life. With minor injuries, she sought refuge in a forest where she was able to meet with other refugees. They remained in hiding until a rumour reached them saying that the war was over. Those brave enough to believe this ventured back to the village and were all killed. **"I have very few memories of my time in hiding,"** she recollects, and thought that she was the only survivor in her family.

Finally the war really was over and at last Donatha was reunited with her brother and sister in the town of Kibuye. They were taken to the JAM Fred Nkunda Orphanage where they were welcomed as part of the family. She was so happy that she did not have to carry the terrible burdens of the last few months alone and was able to be with others who had experienced much the same.

In 1996, it was established that an aunt of Donatha was alive, so she and her brother and sister were fostered into her care. A couple of years later Donatha's aunt sadly passed away and Donatha was offered a full-time position at the Fred Nkunda Life Centre. She is now happy to be a part of changing shattered lives, as was done for her.

"The genocide has completely changed my view of life. I had loving parents who gave me all I needed and they were taken away from me. They spoke about Jesus, but I only came to know him when I arrived at the orphanage. He is now my hope and I hold on to the word in Jeremiah 29:11: 'For I know the thoughts that I think toward you, saith the Lord, thoughts of peace, and not of evil.'"

Welcome home, Donatha.

"*Rwanda will be very nice in the future*"

"There is no problem with my life," says Jean Bosco, *"but sometimes I remember what happened to me and I feel sad and then I immediately go to bed to sleep. I remember the things and get sad quickly when I have problems with someone and when I remember how people were beating my parents.*

"Even if there is nobody there, I would like to go and work in the lands where my parents stayed and get money to progress. I would like to get some animals or start a small business. I want to finish my education, marry and have children.

Jean Bosco grew up with his father, two uncles and his grandfather because his mother died before the war. He was very young when the war started and they ran away.

"I saw many people running away in that time; many ran past our house wearing banana leaves. They were saying that the Rwandans were not of the same tribe. I was separated from my father and brought to the JAM Orphanage. Since then I didn't get any other information about my parents or relatives. I don't think that they can still be alive, because nobody has come to look for me.

Jean Bosco Niyomukiza
Age 16
Born in Buringa, Gitarama.
Region: JAM Orphanage, Gitarama.
Attends P5 in Shyogwe Primary School.

"I don't like to remember what happened. I think that I will be able to forget one day because I don't think about it all the time any more. What makes me happy now is to play. Maybe if I went to stay on a farm, I will be able to forget by working.

"My biggest wish is to have a very good life. Rwanda will be very nice in the future, now that agriculture has started to develop and there are many factories. People also know how to do many technical jobs. Things are different since the war because the Rwandans who were out of the country are coming back to work hard towards a better future for themselves.

Jean Bosco feels that the world should know what happened in Rwanda because when they know, they will see that Rwanda needs to be helped. *"Organisations help people to develop themselves by enabling them to help themselves.*

"It is a good thing to share with each other. When you have a lot of food and you refuse to give to another, there is no interest for you. When you are rich, you have to share with others, because you don't know if you might need help tomorrow and then have to ask others for help."

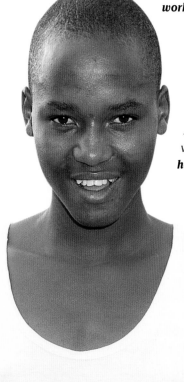

"Conflict is not necessary to resolve situations"

Fiston has been suffering from stomach problems ever since the war and says that he is frustrated and sad when these problems keep him out of school. He likes studying and reading – especially about the war and history of Rwanda. He would like to become a doctor or a journalist, because these occupations both help people. Fiston's father was a doctor before he died.

He describes what happened in the war: *"It was around 8 pm when the President died. It was night and people started to blow whistles loudly all over Kigali. They were shouting that the President had died and that the people had to start killing people to avenge him. I was afraid.*

"I went to hide at a neighbour. My parents were killed while I was there. I was 11 years old, my two sisters were 23 and 21 and my two brothers were 19 and 16 years old. The rest of our family tried to get away, but they met the killers on the way and died.

"About two weeks later, the killers caught my one remaining brother and also killed him. When I remember my family I feel very sad, but I try to chase the thoughts from my mind.

"In this time, the killers were attacking the suspected Tutsi families all over the city, asking for their identification cards. When they found anybody without an ID card, they would immediately kill them.

"I saw this and felt that I was going crazy because after the death of my parents I felt I had no hope of escape. Some killers lived near to us. It seemed that people were not ashamed of killing, regarding it as a game. Friends of my parents brought me food in the evenings when I went to hide on the mountain. I sometimes had to eat uncooked rice soaked in cold water. Some people had bad hearts and some people good hearts."

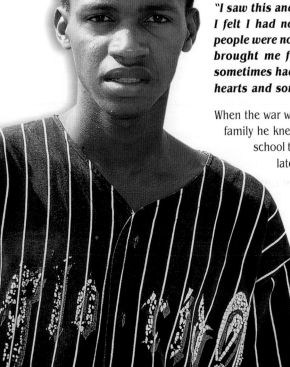

Fiston Nsekanabo
Age 18
Born in Kigali.
He attends ETEM – Ecole Technique du Mukingi S2.

When the war was over Fiston went to a Catholic centre in Kigali where he stayed with a family he knew. After a while they wanted him to stop attending school so one of his school teachers then took him in because he was a very good student. His teacher later took him to the Ministry of Local Government and Social Affairs.

"I presented my problems there. After listening, they said that they would like to put me in an orphanage where I can have a better life and keep studying. This is how I came to JAM in 2000. It makes me very happy to know that I will have a good life in future because it is what God wants for me. I also feel that differences and conflicts between people can be resolved if someone can approach those people and talk to them and try to tell them that what they are doing is not good. Conflict is not necessary to resolve situations."

"God answered my prayers"

Fillette says she is happy with her life now because she has food to eat and somewhere to live. *"My life is not like it was in the forest.*

"I would like to continue with school and get a job. I would like to be a doctor to help other people like the doctors helped me when I was in a bad condition. When I can look after myself I will be able to provide for all my needs and not be dependent on anybody."

Fillette Nyiransabimana
Age 16
Born in Kacyiru.
Region: JAM Orphanage, Gitarama.
Completed P6 and currently attends sewing class in the Technical Training Centre at JAM.

Fillette's mother was a nurse before the war but she doesn't remember where her father worked. *"We had a car. When I think about the war, I think of the living conditions and how I lost my mother. These things make me feel sad and cause me to sometimes think about killing myself.*

"When the war started in Kigali and the militia came, my mother and my baby brother and sister were killed while my father and I were hiding in the ceiling of the house."

They fled to Ruhengeri and had to abandon the car. They hid in a sorghum field for a while but were caught and taken to a house full of other people. The militia set fire to the house. *"My father burned to death but the fire did not get to me because I hid in the toilet with another woman who had a child on her back. We could not leave the house immediately because it was close to the road where the militia were waiting with machetes. I was thinking that it would maybe be better if I also died.*

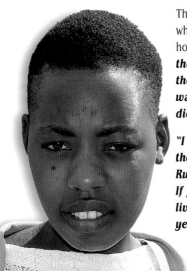

"I went to Gisenyi where a boat took us to Congo. A Congolese nurse saw me in the market and took me to her house to take care of me for a few years. Other Rwandans came there one day and told her: 'You are with a little Rwandan girl. If you don't give her to us, we will come and kill your whole family.' I went to live in the Congolese forest where I hid with many other Rwandans for four years. We only came out to look for food. When the RPA came to fight in the Congo, they came to the forest to look for Rwandans. The ICRC brought me to JAM's Orphanage in August 2001.

"My wish for the future is to get the best life. I am well now. When I get the means to buy something that I need for myself... that is the best life. The other best thing is when you can live peacefully without hearing about fighting.

"I also believe in God, because you leave evils like stealing and adultery and you live in a good way that you follow to heaven. God works among many people and when you get something it is an answer to the many prayers you prayed."

"People in their villages can work together"

Alexis is afraid to leave the orphanage and adapt to life outside. At 16 he realises he needs to be independent and does not see his life ending in the orphanage.

Alexis likes to play football and to study. He says that football sometimes provides a good future for players and would like to reach that level. He plays for the orphanage soccer team.

"I would like to go to secondary school to do nursing, Maths and Physics if I can pass P6. I do quite well at school. I also think about doing a technical course but my dream is to be a professional soccer player."

Alexis came to the JAM Orphanage after the war and says that he still feels sad when he remembers the war, but he tries to be strong when he is alone, and during the annual week of mourning in Rwanda.

"Where I was born, the situation was not like it was in the other areas, because when the killers came to kill us, we tried to defend ourselves. When they saw this they asked others to help them kill us. I kept hiding throughout the war.

"Although the situation was bad in the past, I see that life is improving again. People have started to put the past behind them.

"I feel that to prevent something similar happening again, people should sit together and talk about how to avoid it. When I say people, I mean everybody who has time to talk about it, because anybody can make a difference. People in their villages can work together, chiefs can call all the people together and they can discuss and make good decisions on how to avoid it, because the war killed people and left only orphans, widows and destruction behind."

The only survivor of Alexis' family is his older brother who is a farmer and lives in Bisesero on their parents' land. He would like to be with him so that they could help each other. *"It is bad for me think that we are the only ones left. We are only two people. It could have been better if it were my whole family..."*

Alexis Nzabamwita
Age 16
Born in Bisesero, Kibuye.
Region: JAM Orphanage, Gitarama.
Attends P6 in Shyogwe Primary School.

JAM also cares for abandoned babies

Staff from the Kabgayi Hospital in Gitarama brought Clementine to the JAM Orphanage in March 2001 when she was nine months old. They had been caring for her since she was born and could not take care of her any more.

Her maternal aunt had come to the orphanage to visit her and told her the story. Clementine's father had been killed in a car accident just before her mother died while giving birth to her.

All her family members and relatives had been killed in the genocide. Her story is one of many. The orphanage takes care of many children with similar histories.

The Kinyarwandan word "Harerimana" means "Only God takes care of children."

When Moses came to the Congo in 2000, he was little more than a whimpering baby skeleton. He was brought to the orphanage by a nun working as a social worker at Kabgayi hospital (2 km from the JAM Centre). Moses was found crying, left alone in a bed in the maternity ward. A woman told the nurse that she had seen a lady put a baby in the bed before she disappeared.

The development of his teeth gave his age away. He was 18 months old in a body the size of a four-month-old baby. He was so malnourished that his growth was severely stunted.

When Moses was two years old he was barely able to support his weight on his thin little legs. He is still very small for his age. The staff at the orphanage keep an eye on his eating habits.

Today, Moses is able to run with the other young children and likes to kick a soccer ball. He is still quite uncomfortable on his feet, but has come a long way since we received him. He is friendlier than the other young children and immediately walks toward any stranger who visits the babies at the orphanage.

Many single mothers can't afford to raise their babies so they abandon them at hospitals or on the doorsteps of strangers. The authorities then bring them to the orphanage.

During the war, many babies were separated from their parents or were left in bushes on the roadside because of the difficult journeys families undertook.

Many children were found unaccompanied in the forests. Through NGOs and Government channels, they were brought to JAM's Fred Nkunda Life Centre. Some still stay in the orphanage, others have been reunited with relatives or have moved on and started anew with foster families.

Many of the younger children are often in a severe state of malnourishment. If these children survive, they are placed with foster families and, because they are still young, they seem to adapt quickly and enjoy the special love, safety and security that only a family can offer.

Moses Harerimana
Age: Just over two years old.

Clementine Umuhoza
Age: One year and nine months.
Attends pre-school at JAM Orphanage.

Prematurely aged by the war

Seraphine is 15 years old but looks much older since the war has aged her. She has been robbed of living a normal life.

It was a normal day at home when she and her family were suddenly engulfed by thick smoke. The houses in their village were on fire. Chaos ensued and the villagers began running in all directions. She and her family joined in the chaos and ran to the local district office as soldiers made their presence known. Guns were fired and many people died in a hail of bullets. Many others were able to flee to the forests, however, and when the soldiers finally left, drums were used to signal that it was once again safe to return to the village. People united as they saw the devastation and took refuge on a school playground.

Three days later chaos once again broke out and again people took refuge in the forest, only this time dogs were used to sniff them out. **"I was made to watch as my parents were brutally murdered. My life was spared as the soldiers expected me to die anyway, being as young as I was."**

As Seraphine ran through the forest to her parents' coffee plantation, she came across her sister and uncle. Her uncle left to get a boat that would take them across Kivu Lake to the Congo. He never returned.

"A man later discovered me hiding and offered me refuge in his home. Three months later he returned home from work with a spear in his hand, ready to kill me."

Once again, Seraphine fled and went into hiding. Finally the war ended and she was taken to a refugee camp, where she was reunited with an aunt. She was filled with joy at having a familiar person with her. She explained that her aunt wanted to go back to her house to see if there was anything left to salvage. Seraphine waited for days for her return. Instead, her body was discovered a short distance from her home.

It was originally planned that Seraphine be taken to a local orphanage until someone recommended the JAM Fred Nkunda Orphanage. By being accepted in this wonderful place, Seraphine has been given a second chance in life, with the opportunity of a good education and the closeness of caring staff and friends, who are now her home, her family.

Having spent some years in the JAM Orphanage, Seraphine was asked how she felt towards the soldiers that had so brutally murdered her family. **"I can forgive the killers. I have learnt to trust people again.... I don't have problems talking about the past, even though I don't like it, but when I am asked about the future I get so scared. I am afraid of what is waiting for me when I finally move out the orphanage."**

Seraphine Uwimana
Age 15
Born in Kibuye.
Region: JAM Orphanage, Gitarama.
She is in P4 in Shyogwe Primary School.

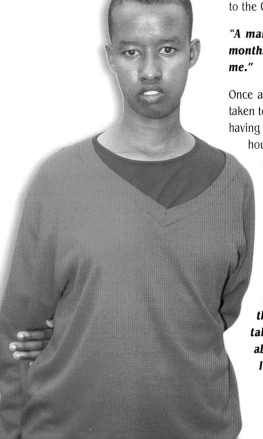

"Sad, not angry"

Delphine says that her life was very good before the war, because her parents gave her all she needed. She was an only child and remembers her mother staying at home and her father running a small business, selling things like pots, sugar and fabrics. She was very close to her mother and saw the business when they went to visit her father.

"One night in 1990, when we were at home, many people came and killed my father. My mother and I locked ourselves in a dark room and survived.

"It was in 1994 when we heard people making a lot of noise outside. We went outside and they told us to come with them to a meeting place in the mountains. We were together until the evening came.

"We saw a big group of people coming towards us, and we all ran in different directions, trying to escape the killers. I got separated from my mother, but I soon met an old lady who took me to her place. The next morning she told me to move on. I was moving around in the mountains for a couple of weeks. Sometimes I spent days in the forests without eating, until I found a family who gave me something to eat.

"Since I lost my parents my life had been quite bad. I visited many people on the way, but they all told me to keep going until I arrived home safely. So I kept on going, spending nights and days on the streets and in the forests."

Delphine spent three years moving from family to family. One day a man took her to the district office and she was brought to the JAM Orphanage in Gitarama.

She says that it is good to be with other children now. She has many friends and likes to play soccer, but would like to be like a child in a family again.

Delphine Uwimana
Age 18
Born in Byumba.
Region: JAM Orphanage, Gitarama.
Currently attending Shyogwe Primary School level 6.

"I want to serve my country, study and contribute by doing the job that I study for. When I improve in sewing, I can fix clothes for people and they can give me money. From this I can give to other people who do not have any. I would also like to help children who don't have means by supporting them. If I meet children on the streets, I will take them home, and care for them if I can. I believe that having a good job is necessary to have a good life.

"When I think about those who killed my family, I only feel sad. I am not angry, because there is nothing I can do to them. Rwanda is improving, because the situation is different now. People were killing each other but now they have started to be reconciled with one another.

"My wish is that I can continue my studies when I go out of the orphanage."

"Through JAM I have good friends"

I"I have been on my own since 1995. I live here in the place where my parents died, because there is no other way or means for me to live in another place. We had neighbours who were of the opposite tribe and wanted to kill us.*

"We went up to a village and when we arrived in the mountains of Bisesero my parents got killed. They just cut them down with pangas and ubuhidis (wooden sticks with a heavy, round end). I saw them die. I even saw my younger brothers, sisters and other relatives die.

"I was left behind alone. On 26 June 1994 I got shot in the leg. I also had problems with my back because I was falling often when I was running. God protected me and I didn't die.

"A child (named Casimir) came to see how I was and I told him: 'Go, because the killers might see you and kill you. I am going to die.' He kept asking me to come with him until I agreed to go. By chance he also survived and we are good friends today, because we were also together at JAM. We left the orphanage together in April 1995.

"Like it was before, and also like it was in the orphanage, I don't have parents and I am alone. My wife was also an orphan in the orphanage.

"I am happy to be back in Kibuye, because there was nowhere else to go. This is the only way I can be. My wife's name is Dative. I was married on 27 December 2001. I met her at the JAM Fred Nkunda Orphanage. We were from the same area and when I came back to Kibuye we decided to help each other because we had the same problems and got married.

"There were people from the JAM Fred Nkunda Orphanage who were lucky to go to school. Others have jobs that are helping themselves.

"Many children who have been at the JAM Orphanage are living the same kind of life as me. Many boys are like me. Girls have been trying to marry to have something to eat. For us, to get married was not because we were grown up enough, but a way of trying to have something to eat or for someone to be with us to help us.

"I also thank JAM because they have been able to employ some children in the orphanage. When I got married, many people helped me and even personally attended my wedding. It made me very happy, because I saw – even though I don't have any brothers or sisters – I have good friends.

"You are among the first of the people who have helped us and saved our lives. You have protected us in a bad and difficult time. Up to now who we are is because of you. You have even seen the life we have now. We ask you what you can do for our children...

"We thank you for seeing the problem and taking the message to people."

Adrien Harorimana
Age 22
Region: Karama, Musenyi, Kibuye.

"I don't know what I should be reconciled with"

"I left the JAM Fred Nkunda Orphanage in 1999 to stay with some relatives in Kibuye. I had to drop out of school because I had to look after the cows every day. They treated me bad and I did not feel like their own child. They did not have any other children but I stayed together with the other workers in the house. Later on I went to the Nyamishaba Orphanage to ask for help, but I was again placed in the same family. I decided to run away and I now live alone."

Felicien stays in a shelter on the land that belonged to his aunt in Bisesero. An NGO helped him to build it when he ran away. There are no doors or windows to keep out the cold in the evenings or the rain during the rainy season. Felicien has many small jobs in the area he lives in and uses the little bit of money he earns for food.

His parents were killed in the genocide after the militia attacked the group they were hiding with. His mother and brother were killed immediately, but he and his father escaped by jumping into a river nearby. Only a few days later, his father lost his life too. Felicien was very scared when he saw his family killed because it was the first time in his life that he had seen dead bodies.

Felicien Nzabamwita

Age: 18 years old.
Date of birth: 1984. Born in Kibuye.
Region: Bisesero, Rusenyi.

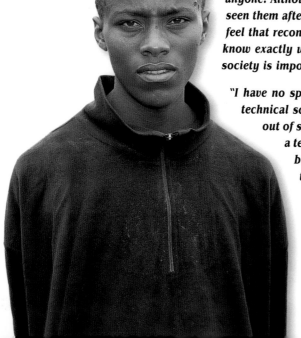

"When I think about the genocide I start thinking about my own life. My parents used to give me everything, but when I face problems today I start thinking about how they were killed. I feel angry when thinking about what happened and some days I think that I will take my own life because I am so discouraged.

"The killers were just like us so I did not understand why they would want to kill us. I don't know who exactly killed my family so I don't want to report anyone. Although I remember the people who killed my mother, I have not seen them after the war and I don't know if I would recognise them today. I feel that reconciliation might take place in Rwanda, but personally I don't know exactly what it is that I should be reconciled with. Reconciliation in society is important to get rid of the division between people.

"I have no specific plans for my future yet, but I would like to attend a technical school if I get means to continue my studies. Because I went out of school I find it difficult to plan for the future, but I hope to get a technical job one day. Most of all I want to become a mechanic, but I am happy to just get a job which can give me some money to buy what I need. I like to do agriculture and can also become a farmer, but my biggest problem is to get means to start digging the land that I live on."

Felicien is happy to have a shelter to sleep in and is thankful to have his own place, even though life can be difficult at times.

"Killing was the work of the devil"

Suleiman helps in the kitchen by preparing food, washing up big pots and running errands for The Centre of Empowerment of Women in Gitarama.

He says that to have a job makes him happy as it helps him live from day to day. He used to study mechanics at technical school but when he was halfway through the course he had to leave as he needed to look for a way of getting food for his brothers and sisters.

He says: *"Because I get some money now, I can buy some things; it has solved some of the problems. I try to buy some decent clothes so that I don't look like a street boy. I believe that cleanliness is very important, however poor you are in life. I have two brothers and I am responsible for them.*

"We try to grow food for the market and work on the land that we have. My brothers work on the land at home unless they can get jobs outside, like the one I have now. They do not attend school. They were studying but both stopped because there was no food to eat.

"I am the head of my family now and am in charge of everything. There is no other adult in my family left to help us, as a result of the war.

"Many things in the country were destroyed in the war. Before the war, people were sharing what they had and were even giving cows to each other. But now it seems that everybody is looking after himself. The friendship which was there before is not the same today.

"I grew up not knowing about tribes. I just knew that people were the same but because of bad leadership, bad political issues were taught to the people. Instead of one nation, people started to see two types of people. One became a Tutsi and the other became a Hutu. I believe that is how and when the devil created killing between people.

"My mother and sister survived the war, but when they went home, a lady put poison in their food. They both died.

"We knew the woman who poisoned our mother from before the war and when we heard the bad news, we felt very sad. I felt like reporting the women to the court, but afterwards I heard that God will punish the sinners. The word of God says that we should forgive those who have broken our hearts. We had nothing else to do so I just kept quiet.

"My biggest wish today is to study and have a job. Life changes according to how the days also change, but if I go ahead with studies it can help me improve."

Suleiman Mahoro
Age 24
Born in Gitarama.
Completed S1 in secondary school.

"I buried my own parents"

"I could not continue at school because of a lack of means. At my age it can be good if I can go to a technical school to acquire a skill.

"In the orphanage we were given food daily, but we saw that it would be good for us if we could look for food for ourselves. When I came here to Ngoma, I was very happy to find my older brother still alive. Our job now is to dig the land to get food to stay alive. The land that we work on is ours, but we are living in a rented house, because our houses were destroyed and we don't have means to rebuild the houses.

"My brother is supporting me. We have some other relatives, but they don't help us in any way. They have never helped me with shoes or trousers – everybody is trying for himself now. The love in people has become very little but at least we have enough food to survive.

"I can say that if I go beyond the age of going to school, I can get married and start another life, but I am still young. That is why if another person can help me it will be so helpful.

"We saw people coming to burn houses, saying that it was the Tutsi tribe that had killed the President. They felt that they should exterminate this tribe with all their traditional weapons.

"People destroyed our houses and took our animals. Others were also coming to take our crops from the garden. We had to run away to the forests to save our lives.

"Some people were shot, some cut down with pangas and others burnt while the rest were merely running away. People who were not being cut down with traditional weapons were dying of hunger. If you did not die of hunger, you died of disease. There was an epidemic and people were dying because it was raining a lot. I cannot mention all the things that were killing the people during this period of three months.

"I heard from other people when my parents died. I buried them myself. Other people also came to help me bury the bodies. I used to visit the place where I buried my parents, but I don't go there any more because it makes me think about many things.

"I don't know what to think about the people who did these things. We never even knew why it had happened. I still don't know the reason, but when I think about it, I see it was like a lesson so that people will not kill each other again. I see that it is good to fight against it and to have self control to avoid it from happening again."

Innocent Muhayimana
Age 18
Born in Gitabwa, Kibuye.
Now lives with his brother and his
brother's wife in Ngoma, Kibuye.
Finished P5.

Rose Mukamudenge
Age 39
Married to Aaron Kabogora with three children.
Completed P2 in 1979.

"I had a heart for caring for children"

Rose originally lived at the JAM Fred Nkunda Orphanage because she was badly wounded during the war. The staff at the orphanage looked after her and took care of her many children at that time. She lost a few of her children in the genocide and later remarried once the war was over, and now has a total of three children.

"During the war I had been beaten all over my body with traditional arms. I had even been stabbed in my back with traditional spears. I have scars all over my body. I have been chopped with machetes and hit in my leg with a stick that had nails driven through it. I still have a nail embedded in the bone of my leg. Fred (the founder of the JAM Orphanage) came and took the children from the camp where we were all together, and saw I was also in a bad situation and so asked me to go with him too. At the orphanage, they put me in a quiet place to get better. They kept me in a separate room with a basin. I used to wet a towel and put it around my head to break the fever I had. My whole body was infected. They also gave me some of the medicine that they had been giving the children.

"Fred gave me 17 children to look after and they were happy to be with me because they did not like to have young girls look after them. I needed to keep helping other children as Fred also helped me. I did everything for them. I washed them and their clothes. Even today, I get headaches when I have to carry something on my head.

"I had gone through many difficulties and even lost my own children. I had a heart for caring for children, because God had protected me in the war. Because this person decided to receive me in the orphanage, I also wanted to help the children that God helped to survive. When I left the orphanage with my younger brother, the people did not want to see me go. I got married later to my current husband."

Rose was previously married before the war, but lost her husband, son and five-year-old daughter in the genocide. Rose spent two months living naked in a ditch during the April rain, after seeing her daughter's head being beaten to a pulp with a hoe and a stick with nails driven through them.

"When I think about the war, I do not know what can stop it from happening again. I know the problems that I went through, but I believe in God and I do not believe that it will happen again. My three girls' names are Mukeshimana Jacqueline (six), Uwamahoro Alphonsine (four) and Mukamwiza Immaculee.

"I wish for them to grow up, have a good life and to go to school. This depends on money that we will have to get. We may need help to go to school so that their future life can be good.

"My brother is alive and he used to come and visit me, but he is also busy with his life. He had a problem one day when somebody gave him 12 cows to take care of and they were struck by lightning. It killed all of them. Even the man who was helping them is suffering today like us. We don't know what to think of disasters like this..."

"*I need to stay in Rwanda to support it*"

I clean a restaurant and take food for other customers, or buy things for the restaurant. I do this full time now and had to stop studying because I didn't have food to eat. I was unhappy to stop studying, but I got a job immediately.

"There are some people who are very rich and the poor start to get poorer. When you look bad and walk down the road, some relatives see you and say: 'Look, this orphan. He is bad, even though he has someone that looks after him.' I don't want people not to respect me, because of the way I look. If people see that you are dirty, they think bad things of you, but when you look smart, they tell you that you are smart.

"I am happy with my life because it is better now, but it could be even better if I had more money and if I could do some business. When I think in my heart about my future, I would like to be rich one day, because you can also make your family rich if they are poor. It is good to help them. My father died when I was a baby. I heard from other people that he had heart disease. When he was working he fell down and died. I stay with my two older brothers because we are still young, but when I grow up, I would like to get my own house and a wife.

"I like people who do good things and who are friendly. I also like money. There are friends that you like and others that you love. When you share with your friends, they sometimes help you to be strong. When I think about the war, I remember what happened to the people that were killed – but we forget, because it is in the past.

"When you have a friend and you start to see division between you, it can be a critical situation. Sometimes you have a friend for three years, and someone can come and put division between you. War starts when there are problems between countries – some people run away, while some die in the war. I listened to people that said that when a Hutu sees a Tutsi, he has to kill him. People don't talk like this any more. There was hatred inside people at that time. I am happy that I don't know anybody like this now.

"I like Rwanda because it is my nation. I need to stay here to support it, because I was born here. For example, I can make a difference in my country by composing a song for Rwanda. When it is played over the radio, people can benefit from my words. I can sing that I love God because He protects me. Other people can also see that it is true and that He also protects us all. I like to sing when I am happy, especially the worship songs.

"The most important thing in my life is to help others when I grow up. I would like to give something to people who are poor. I would also like to take care of the people who are handicapped. I care about those people because they cared about me."

Joseph Musengamana

Age 15
Region: Stays in Rugarama, Gitarama with an older brother.
Completed P3 last year in Rugarama Primary and is currently a cleaner/waiter in a restaurant in Gitarama.

"I can forgive the killers because it is finished"

"I have a life, but it is not very good. It is improving slowly but slowly. I just keep studying because I like it. It is good, because you get knowledge that can help you in the life outside. I like sport and I am happy when I am with other children.

"I don't get materials for school and lose time. Sometimes, I can stay for two weeks at home waiting for school materials. It bothers me a lot when I see other children going to school when I can't.

"My uncle, who is very old and was shot in the chest in 1994, has to help me with school materials. He is handicapped because of this wound and is unable to use the land well. He cannot even produce enough food to live on.

"We were all living together before the war. We were living with my mother, my younger brothers and my uncles.

Thomas Rutebuka
Age 18
Born in Bisesero, Kibuye.
S1 in Esapan School, Kibuye.

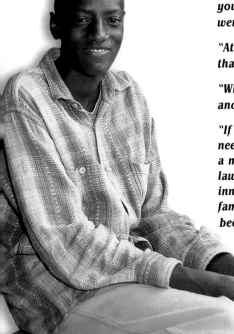

"When the genocide started, everybody was trying to save his or her life by spreading out over the countryside. In the evenings we all had to come together. When you saw someone not coming to the gathering in the evenings, you knew that they had died. In the evenings we were also trying to bury the people who had died. We couldn't dig very deep; we were just covering their bodies with some ground.

"There are many family members whose bodies I had not even seen, because I did not know where they died and if you tried to look for them, you were thinking that you could also get killed along the way. I only saw my mother and my younger brothers die. The rest were killed in the mountains. In these evenings I went around asking: 'Have you found my people? Have you found my people?'

"At the end of the war, people were traumatised and were scared of everything that was making a noise, thinking that the war was happening again.

"When I sit and think and remember how my life was when I was getting clothes and compare it to now, I wonder if this will happen again.

"If I study and get knowledge I can work for my country. I can also cover my needs and can try to develop the country. If I study more, I would like to become a minister or a parliament member. I would like to go to university and study law and education. If I become a lawyer, I want to help people, especially the innocent ones, and punish the criminals. I do not know exactly who killed my family, because there were many people involved. I can forgive them nonetheless, because it is finished.

"If I have one big wish, it is to study, and after my studies, if I get means, to build a house and to start a family. My only problem now is getting clothes. When I look at how well dressed other children are, and compare it to how I am now, this affects my studies."

"I have a good relationship with God"

"My parents were farmers with animals in Kigali before their deaths. We were normal citizens who grew our own food. I went to stay with my uncle in December 2001. The tracing agencies found him in Bisesero and he accepted to look after me. I am happy to be with them.

"I don't know if I will have problems later to find school materials because when you tell them about school, they do not realise how important it is. I do well in school at the moment and the courses are very easy for me. I would like to become a mechanic one day and open my own workshop.

"Bisesero is very deep in the countryside and the people are not interested in playing games like they are in Kigali. There are only men and their wives here in Bisesero and the men only look after their cows. Many young boys were killed in the genocide and when I want to play, I do not have anybody to play with here in Bisesero. The children who are here were born after the war and are still very young.

"If I talk about the problems of the war, I cannot finish all of them. Sometimes when they wanted to kill me, I was lying among dead bodies and smeared blood on my skin to disguise myself. When they were burning the bushes I was hiding in, we used to try and stop the fire with our hands so that it could not reach us. There are so many things, that I cannot mention everything.

" I remember seeing people die. I remember everything. I remember how people's heads were chopped with pangas – especially the women. I saw people being killed with spears. They were even cutting off the genitals of the men. They cut babies from the stomachs of their pregnant mothers. Some people were thrown in ditches and then set alight and some people were thrown into toilets.

"Because I knew how to pray, I asked God to protect me every day. When they were running behind us and I was jumping over the bodies of people, I sometimes also wished that they would kill me. Sometimes I saw many people being killed and no one survived. Some people walked in front of bullets so that they could die quickly instead of being cut or murdered more gruesomely. It was only God who protected me. I remember one time when we were 10 people together and they threw a grenade at us. The grenade killed everyone and they all fell on me, but I was unharmed.

"I have a good relationship with God today. Whenever I have a problem, I pray. I am not scared of my future, even if a war should happen again. I would like to study to become a mechanic and open my own workshop.

"Many Rwandans know how to use computers and many people are educated because of the Government. Before, a Tutsi could not get educated, but now the tribes are the same because the divisions disappeared in the war."

Jean Damascene Ruzibiza
Age 17
Born in Bisesero, Kibuye.
Attends Esapan School, Kibuye.

Still uncertain about the future

"I dream of being a professional soccer player: that is all I want in life at the moment." In the same breath he says he would also like to be a soldier: *"I'm not afraid of death, I'll die one day anyway, so if I die in the war that's OK. I would like to be a soldier who protects my country."*

Like many of the children, he has uncertainty about the future as there are threats of another war starting: *"I fear that the war will break out again. I hear rumours about people fighting in different places."*

He recalls the terrible war in 1994, when he was only nine years old. One evening a few neighbours and soldiers approached Jean's parents' home. Jean went outside and asked how he could help them. They demanded he call his parents outside, but he refused. His refusal caused them to beat him on the head with a panga before being chased away. The soldiers brought his parents outside and killed them. Their bodies were thrown into the river.

It seemed the soldiers were only interested in killing his parents. This gave Jean, his brother and sister a chance to run to the nearby forest, but it wasn't long before the soldiers began their search for the children. Undiscovered for a whole week, the children continued to hide, the only food being a few sweet potatoes they found nearby – hardly the sustenance one would need for the terrible cold nights. Jean and the children decided it was time to move on to another forest – here they were discovered by soldiers. They managed to escape, but with serious injury to his sister. After a short while the two boys went back and found that their sister had survived. The boys sat with her in the bushes where she was lying, not knowing what to do.

Fortunately the children were found by friendly soldiers. They were taken to a military camp where they stayed for about six weeks. The soldiers finally took Jean and his family to the authorities and they were brought to the JAM Fred Nkunda Orphanage. At last some stability had returned to their lives. The children were reunited with distant relatives after spending three years at the orphanage. The situation did not remain a happy one, though, and Jean and his brother returned to JAM's Orphanage where they now attend school and live with their large family – the orphans. Jean enjoys playing the sport he loves most: soccer.

Jean Turatsinze
Age 16
Born in Mytsindji, Rwanda.
Region: JAM Orphanage, Gitarama.
Attends Shyogwe Primary School, level 5.

Jean Claude "Puma" Uwizeyimana
Age 22
Born in Kamazuru, Butare.
Currently stays 4km from the JAM Orphanage,
Gitarama.
Completed S1 in Secondary School.
Goalkeeper in junior team for Gitarama province.

Jean Claude sets out his goals

A supervisor at the orphanage who saw Jean Claude playing soccer gave him the nickname 'Puma', since he reminded him of a South American goalkeeper. The nickname stuck and since Jean Claude left the orphanage everybody in Gitarama has called him 'Puma'.

"Before the war, I was playing soccer for a team in my primary school. I was interested in soccer and I had an older brother at home who also played football and encouraged me to play soccer. I used to see him in the holidays when I came home from school. He played for one of the teams in Gitarama. Sadly, this brother of mine died in the war. I miss him and I am sad that he died, but there is nothing that I can do about it. When I think back on these times, I do not feel happy, but I am so thankful to him for giving me the idea of doing what I am doing today.

"The war started when I was in S1. After that I could not go back to school as I had no money. I went to JAM in 1996. A tracing team was looking for my family at this time and I was reunited. When I arrived in the family, I saw that it would not be possible to study any more. This was my stepmother that I considered as my mother. I have one sister. There are about 12 people staying here. She is a teacher and the salary she gets helps us at home. Because she is very old, the salary she gets will not be there forever. That is why we need to learn something to help us in future to also be able help our younger brothers and sisters.

"When I left the orphanage I was selected for the junior team of the Gitarama Province. JAM used to enter championship soccer teams and we were one of the teams who did well. Because I was still young, everybody was interested to know how I played and who I was. Everybody knew about me when I left JAM and they all wanted me to go and play for them.

"Sport is very good, because it helps you to develop. There are soccer players from Rwanda that have had successful careers playing overseas. In my mind I am planning this, but my club is still at a low level. At the moment I am going to different garages to help qualified mechanics, who are teaching me. I enjoy this very much.

"When the war started I was living in Butare. I did not know what was happening, because I was still very young. It was only when I grew up that I realised what had happened here.

"What I remember is just seeing some bodies lying around and people killing each other because of the orders from their leaders. That time it was only killing and shedding blood. Nothing happened at that time that built up the country.

"I feel sad and feel sorry that all the people died. When your friends die, you feel sad and, moreover, some of those that died were relatives. A person cannot forget something like this. It is not up to any person to decide whether to forget or not."

Sole survivor

Samuel likes to play football and volleyball and loves to swim in Lake Kivu which separates Rwanda from the Democratic Republic of Congo.

"I am in the category of children who can live independently, because I don't have any family left after the war."

An NGO has placed him on a waiting list for a house that is just one kilometre from his place of origin. He feels more secure to live close to his original home so that he can ensure that nothing is taken away from his heritage. He plans to work the land his parents had in order to make some money for his daily living. He is excited to take over all these responsibilities so that he can begin to help himself in supplying for his needs.

"We were five children, mother and father before the war. We were farmers and it was a good life. On one Saturday people starting killing and others started running away from their homes. During the war, every morning at 4 am, if there was something to eat, we were eating. From 6:30 am for the whole day, we were moving from one area to another. My family also died in these groups while they were running around."

All Samuel's relatives died within the first month of the genocide, except his older brother who died three days before the war ended.

"It is impossible for me not to think about the war, because I cannot forget about it. When I think about it, I feel sad in my heart. I am only happy that God saved me from other people who were stronger than me. It is necessary that everybody should forgive, because it is up to God to punish or avenge. If people love each other the country will not face conflicts among themselves.

"There is no good thing in a war. There is only destroying and killing in a war. People only get separated and countries get destroyed. Before, I did not know that I would start and manage my life alone like I now plan to live it. There is no benefit from a war and everybody should prevent it."

Samuel feels that educated people should prevent ignorance in his country by helping to emancipate others who did not have opportunities. He would like to finish secondary school and go to university if he finds *"some kind of financial project"* to help him to pay for his education. He believes that he will have a good future because he prays to God to plan for him.

Samuel Bayingana
Age 16
Born in Ngoma, Gishyita, Kibuye.
In process of being relocated to Gishyita
by IRC.
Attends S2 in Esapan School.

Head of the family – at 17

Francine says that before the war she had a good life because she was living with her parents. She remembers that she was very happy.

"When the war started in 1994 the militia came to kill my father. My mother took us children with her and ran away to hide in the mountains. People were running out of the village and into the mountains to try to get over the border to Burundi."

Once the Bukuru family crossed the border into Burundi a relief organisation supplied them with a tent and a little food and helped them settle into a refugee camp. They remained there for almost a year, until it was safe enough to return to Rwanda. In that year their lives were miserable and uncertain, not knowing whether any of their family had survived or what their future held. Finally, they were able to return home, only to find it totally destroyed. They happened to come across an empty house and so they moved in. With the promise of a normal life Francine was happy once again, but later her happiness was shattered after just a few days of returning.

Her mother sadly fell ill and died. Francine's aunt, her only surviving relative, helped her and her brothers and sisters bury their mother. Later, her aunt took all the children to the JAM Orphanage as she was poor and unable to provide for all of them.

We know very little about young Francine, as she is one of many children who try all they can to forget the haunting memories of the atrocities of the war. We do know however, that Francine would one day like to be a nurse as she wants to be able to help others.

It was in September of 2001 that Francine's aunt passed away. This was a very sad occasion for her as she was the only living adult relative the children had. She now feels it is her responsibility to take care of her five brothers and sisters who are with her in the orphanage. She is scared of the responsibility of looking after them all when they are old enough to leave the orphanage. Even though Francine continues to live a life of uncertainty day to day, without having dream or vision about the future, there is an occasional flicker of hope in her eyes: *"I believe that God will help me to succeed and help others in the best way possible. God is the only one who can help me."*

Francine Bukuru
Age 17
Born in Kibungu Province.
Region: JAM Orphanage, Gitarama.
Attends Ecole Agri Veternaire School, S1, Shyogwe.

A house for Modeste

Modeste stayed at the JAM Fred Nkunda Orphanage before he moved to boarding school during the new school term. The IRC (International Rescue Committee) are building houses for various independent adolescent orphans, so he is waiting for his own house to be built by this organisation.

"This is good action for me, because I was wondering where I was going to be after the orphanage. By all means you have to leave the orphanage at some time, so that I can think for myself about my life, and not somebody else for me.

"I like all my subjects at school, because I don't fail often. I like French, English and Maths.

"I often think about my future and my life and see that it is something difficult. Even when they have finished building my house, I don't know how I will stay there. I don't know if I will go to the house straight from school without anybody that I know in the area. The people are mainly those who were there in the area who killed our families."

Modeste is sceptical about reconciliation in Rwanda because he feels that the killers involved in the genocide will always see him as a threat. Even though he has forgiven the people who killed his loved ones, he feels that many people don't understand reconciliation, and doesn't believe that it will take place within the borders of Rwanda.

"Normally I don't think about the things of the war, because people used to teach us that we have to try to forget about it. I even cry and refuse to talk when I think about it."

Modeste describes the war as **"a confusion"** for him that was something beyond anyone's imagination or comprehension.

"I was injured while we were running in the forests and people were shooting at us. Some people were falling all over. I was also hit by a bullet in the upper body. I kept going, but fell down because of exhaustion. The militia ran past me because they thought that I had died. In the evening a boy, who was also shot in the arm, came and took me to a destroyed house without a roof. After that I just hid in the bushes while the other people were running around.

"It is not my own doing that I survived the war, because I was a very young child. Many other strong boys died. It was only God who did it.

"I am happy to at least get a house without struggling too much. The house where I will go and stay is where I was born. There is at least land that I can use. I am happy that I can at least go to my own house in the holidays."

Modeste Gatayisire
Age 16
Born in Gishyita, Rusenyi, Kibuye.
Region: In process of being relocated to Gishyita by IRC.
Attends S3 in Imena College, Runyinya, Butare.

Sport helps to heal the memories

"My life now is neither bad nor good because the family I stay with are poor. I think that the children who stay in rich families have a much better life than me, but I am happy to stay with my sister because I don't have anywhere else to go."

When Pierre is not at school he looks after his sister's cows and hopes to have his own one day. He dreams of becoming a principal of a school because he believes that education can help people get a better life.

He has many friends from the area and they play volleyball and soccer together. Pierre utilises these sports to relax him from the fears and memories he has of life.

"I went to the JAM Orphanage in 1994 because I did not have anywhere to go and I did not know anyone to take care of me. I went to the orphanage with my sister, but she left before me. My older brother stays in Mwendo with other relatives. We hid together in the war. He never explained to me what was going on, but I remember that many people came to our village wanting to kill us. We ran into a neighbour's house and she hid us there during the war. Because we were hiding in the house, I did not see many people being killed. I don't even remember when I got separated from my parents or how they were killed.

Pierre Habimana
Age 13
Born in Kibuye.
Region: Nyabisiga, Mwendo.
Attends Primary 5, Mubuga School, Bisesero.

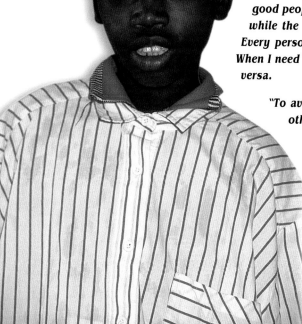

"My sister took me from the orphanage when I was in primary school level one. I wished to stay in the orphanage because I did not have to work hard, but I could play with my friends instead. In JAM I was never sick and I got what I needed there.

"I like to stay in Rwanda. However, there are some bad people and some good people. The good people in Rwanda are the ones who help others, while the bad people don't reach out to help people who are in need. Every person in Rwanda needs someone around them to feel complete. When I need something I can go to my friend and he will help me and vice versa.

"To avoid another war in Rwanda people should learn to help each other and to live together in harmony.

"I don't think that the rest of the world knows about what happened during the genocide. Many people outside Rwanda believe that just a few people were killed and they don't really understand what actually took place in 1994. I think that it is important that the world should know the true history of Rwanda."

"I want to help other people"

"I like to study and I would like to become a doctor because I want to help other people. I live in Ngoma, which is a rural area. Many people need medical assistance because there are many illiterate people here and they don't see the importance of going to hospital when they get sick. They try to heal themselves with traditional medicines. These rural areas need good educated doctors to help them and teach them the importance of professional help.

"I don't know if I will reach my goal because I don't know if I will have the means to pay for the rest of my studies. I don't want to plan further than secondary school because I don't know what challenges I will face in the future. My hope is that I will succeed, and continue my studies at university.

"After the war in 1994 I went to the JAM Fred Nkunda Orphanage in Gitarama where I was living with many other children. I was only a little boy when I came to the orphanage and I was still very sad and discouraged, thinking about what happened in the war. We had an easy life there. The orphanage helped me in many ways. They encouraged me to forget about the war and to concentrate on my studies. If I had not gone to the orphanage I could have ended up as a street boy, living in the city and begging for food. When I think about the street children I feel sorry for them because they have no one to help them and to care for them.

"Organisations like JAM and IRC are very important because they help us so much. If they stop helping us we have to look after ourselves and our lives will become very difficult. However, I will try to do my best to get a good life for myself."

Evaliste says that he has tried to forget the most terrible moments of the war, but every time he faces difficulties he starts thinking about the things that happened in the genocide.

His mother, three sisters and younger brother were all killed by the militia and Evaliste hid with his father. He, too, was later killed.

"I was very young and I did not believe that my father would die because he was so big and strong. Then when he was killed I didn't know what to do and I was very discouraged and sad. Even up to this day I feel terrible when thinking about what happened to my family in the war. However, I try to do good things and I really want to put it in the past and to live on.

"I have forgiven the killers after the war. Some of them have realised what they actually did in the war and they have repented. I feel sad when thinking about what they did to the people I love, but I think I have forgiven them."

Evaliste Habinshuti

Age 17
Born in Kibuye.
Region: Ngoma, Rusenyi.
Attends Esapan Secondary School, level 2.

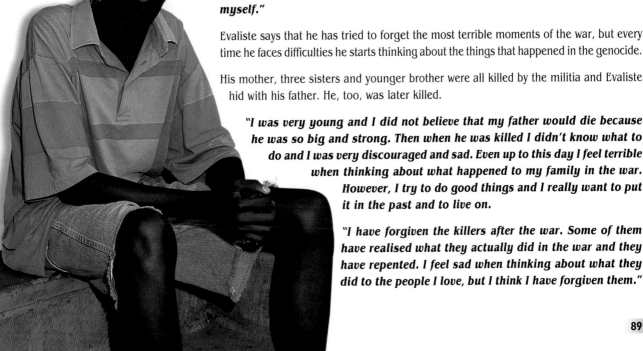

"Education changes the minds of people"

Fabien has moved out of the Kibuye Orphanage which recently closed down. During the holidays he will stay with some of the other children who also had to move out. Together they share a ruined house, but this is just temporary. The IRC are building houses for them and will help to integrate them into society.

Fabien says: *"I was happy in the orphanage because I was together with other children. But I am both excited and scared about starting a new life outside the orphanage. I am happy to get my own house but I think it will be difficult to get means to go back to school again."*

He wants to go to university and continue to study to become a teacher.

"As a teacher you have to learn to live together with all kinds of people. Education changes the minds of people and makes them intellectual. Education is very important for children in Rwanda.

"I think that the people who were involved in the genocide killed people because of ignorance and lack of education, but I have forgiven them.

"I hope that reconciliation will take place one day because if a genocide will happen again I don't know what will happen to our country. It is necessary to eliminate the possibility of people trying to kill each other again. I think that people have learnt a lesson from the genocide and that they will never dare to do something like this again. Both I, who was a victim in the war, and the killers have all suffered different consequences from the war.

"I have hopes for my future, and believe that it will be better. I think that God saved me so that I could survive the war. I don't know how I possibly could have survived all those killings. My biggest wish now is to continue my studies because I need education to survive.

"The country suffered because we lost so many people in the war. We lost educated people and old people who used to teach the children about the history of Rwanda."

During the first week of April each year he thinks a lot about his parents. This was the last time he had contact with them.

"We remember how we lived in the war and it is important for people in Rwanda to be reminded about what happened to their families. It is also important for the world to know what happened in Rwanda in 1994. If I can give some advice, I want them to know that all people are the same and everybody's lives have the same worth."

Fabien Hategekimana
Age 19
Born in Kibuye.
Region: Rusenyi, Gishyita.
Attends Institute Presbyterian Kerinda,
Secondary 4. (Teaching section)

Wants to teach computer studies

"When I left the JAM Orphanage I came to Bisesero and I had a bad life. I could not continue my studies and had to stay out of school for two years. After two years I decided to go to an orphanage in Kibuye to ask for help. I later left there to stay with my brother, who got handicapped in a car accident.

"My first plan is to finish my studies. I will try to get a job, but there are few opportunities in this area. Many people have no or little education and they only get what they can from digging the ground. I struggle to get money to buy my school materials because my brother doesn't have a job because of his handicap.

"I want to finish my Mathematics and Physics courses. When I finish those, I would like to learn to use the computer. I also dream of going to university to continue my studies after secondary school. I want to become a teacher because there are so few qualified teachers in the secondary schools in Rwanda. If I learn to use the computer I would like to teach students in this area. If you learn to use the computer the students can get many different kinds of jobs. I also want to teach in Physics and Mathematics as well. Physics and Mathematics are important courses because they can help the future leaders to design projects in order to develop the country.

"I think that Rwanda will be developed in the future. More children are studying today than before the war and I think that they will work together to build our country in the future.

"I like Rwanda because it is not the country itself that killed my parents, but the people who live here. I see that reconciliation has started in Rwanda, but I think that many of the people who were involved in the genocide are afraid and are not willing to come and ask for forgiveness. Maybe they feel that reconciliation is not possible because we will never forgive them. They are ashamed when they meet many of the people whom they tried to kill. They want to escape because they believe that we have evil thoughts towards them.

"I will forgive the killers if they truly repent and ask for forgiveness from the depths of their hearts. I don't know if reconciliation is possible because the people who were involved in the genocide still have their families while the victims are left without anybody to care for them. The victims will always be reminded about what was done to them because of their loss."

Innocent Havugimana
Age 20
Born in Bisesero.
Region: Bisesero, Kibuye.
Attends Ecole de Droit et Administration
Secondary School in Birambo, level 3.

Christine Kampire
Age 15
Born in Buringa Commune, Gitarama.
Attends S2 at Shyogwe Secondary School.

"*Focus on likeness more than differences*"

After Christine became an orphan as a result of the genocide, she lived in orphanages for about six years and was finally reunited with her older sister, with whom she now lives. Christine is happy to be able to go to one of the best schools in Gitarama. She often discusses with her friends things that can help them forget about their past and the war, such as studies, games and life at school.

Although Christine has friends, life at school is difficult at times. She is often called bad names and there is a perception that most orphans are HIV positive, which adds to the pressure of these children's daily lives.

"The children at school harass me because I am an orphan. They want to show me that I am different from them and that they are better than me."

When the war started, Christine was living at home with her father and three sisters. Her mother died when she was seven years of age. Both her father and a sister were murdered at home, and she was made to watch it all happen. Christine's life was spared because of her age, and one of the soldiers responsible for the death of her father and older sister forced Christine to go home with him and work hard in his house.

"Two weeks after I had been with this soldier, militia came looking for the people who were responsible for killing so many. The soldier became afraid and lifted his panga to end my life but I was rescued just before I was struck."

After a period of being moved from one place to another, Christine was reunited with her younger sister. This gave her much joy as she had thought she was the only survivor. The two of them were finally placed in the JAM Orphanage in Kapgai, which was originally located in old school buildings. Once the schools were reopened, they were moved to the new building in Gitarama.

The JAM Orphanage treated her well and she felt that the staff took care of all the children as they would their own. One day, Christine would like to go to university to study Chemistry and possibly become a doctor but, like some children, she is haunted by death and doesn't know whether she will live long enough to do this. Christine says that should she be lucky to live a long life, she would like to help other orphans or needy children.

"I want to study and become clever so that I can help Rwanda. I would like to help children who are disturbed because of the genocide. I want to encourage Rwandan people to focus on likeness more than differences."

Mimi Habimana
Age 13
Born in Gihara.
Region: Kibuye.
Attends Mushabati Primary School, level 3.

"I would like to be a hero in my country"

Mimi stayed with his sister at the JAM Orphanage until 1999. They later moved to another orphanage in Kibuye and stayed there for quite some time. Again, they moved to the land of their parents in Mushabati after the orphanage closed down and lived in a shelter on the land. His sister died two months later. He now stays with his 16-year-old cousin, Bernard, and another orphan from the JAM Orphanage in a rented house in Kibuye town. His biggest wish is to obtain a better place to live and to have food to eat and clothes to wear.

"The life at JAM was good because we got enough food and clothes, and the staff were nice to me. I miss the life at the orphanage and sometimes dream of going back. If I could manage to buy a ticket for the taxi and if I could find the way back to Gitarama I would like to go back.

"Before the war I had a happy life, but when the war started my parents were killed and I became an orphan. I was only five years old in 1994 and my sister used to carry me on her back. She used to say to me that if she got killed I had to run away and hide so that I would not die. My sister, Bernard and I survived the war by hiding in bushes.

"One day some killers found us and asked us to show them other people who were hiding in the bushes. We led them away from the people that were hiding around us and told them that many people were hiding on the other side of the mountain. When they had gone we met some Catholic sisters who took us to their church in Kibuye. We stayed there through the rest of the war. I was very happy when the war ended – I was still alive. I am thankful to God that He protected me during the war.

"When I grow up I want to help my country. Not all the killers are in prison. Some of them are still hiding in the forests or have run away. If I join the army we can try to find the killers and fight against them. I would like to be a hero in my country and become a soldier in the army to avenge what they did to my family in the war. I don't think much about the future and I don't care whether I die or live. Sometimes I even think that the war can happen again some day.

"If I were to give a message to everybody, I would tell them about God and how He can help us. If everybody starts praying, the genocide will not happen again. I believe in Him because He protected me during the war."

Pedalling towards a better future

Minani operates a bicycle taxi in Kibuye town. He hires his bicycle for 400 francs per day and averages 100 francs profit each day. He told us how business has been quiet as there have been few customers lately compared to the normal everyday trading. He would like to get his own bicycle one day once he has earned enough to purchase it. A used bicycle can cost up to 22,000 Rwandan francs each, so the financial outlay is large for his business.

"Life is difficult for all of us. You must have money to have a good life. The money I make now is only enough to eat from and I cannot buy shoes or clothes. This is the same for everybody who were orphans, because they also don't have means or anything to start with. It will make Rwanda a good country when they help all the orphaned children who are living in the streets, so that everybody can at least have a foundation.

"One day I went to visit my 12-year-old brother who was adopted by a parliament member. When he saw me, he was astonished to see me. He said that he thought that we as orphans had already been helped. When he saw me, he asked: 'Didn't you buy anything like clothes with the money they gave you?' I told him that we didn't get any help. My younger brother is looked after well, but I don't see him often because he lives in Kigali. The parliament member has adopted three other children and when I go there I try not to make the other children upset with my brother because he has a relative who visits him. They have a better life than I have, but it is better to have your own family because there is nobody that can compare to your own father and mother.

"It is good for my brother to be there. When the militia killed my mother in the stadium here in Kibuye, I had him on my back. He doesn't even know anything about our relatives. He is very fond of me. It made me happy to have my brother with me in the war. I don't like to remember what happened in the war. It is like a mental torture for me to talk about the things that happened in the war because what happened, happened. To keep talking about how my family died and who killed them and how I saw their bodies lying on the ground, has no benefit. When I don't have benefit or anything that can come out of my words, it doesn't make me happy. I even sometimes think about committing suicide.

"Even now I see prisoners in the street who may have killed my mother." (In Rwanda the prisoners do community service like fetching water or maintaining roads under armed guard.) *"When I think of them, I just pray that God can help them.*

"I sometimes miss the children from JAM. I even meet some of them around. We are friends. We sometimes discuss the things we did when we were in the orphanage. When we remember the toys we had, we miss them and wish that we could have the same things. We only have good memories from that time. We still talk about things like the roller-skates we used to play with."

Anastase Minani
17 years
Born in Gacaca.
Region: Rubengera, Kibuye.
Currently living in Kibuye town.
Completed P4.

"People have changed and have good hearts"

"I am in secondary level four and have chosen to become a teacher because I want to teach the children in my area. I want to try to encourage the children in Bisesero to go to school, and show the importance of education in order to have a good life. My village needs education because they need to change their minds. Not only the children, but also the adults need to learn how to do good things instead of bad things. If the children who grow up today go to school, they will develop the village and they will improve our living conditions."

Speciose married in August 2001 and lives with her husband in Bisesero. She told us how important it is to her to start a family because she had lost her own through the genocide. But first, she wants to finish school.

She was separated from her family as the war spread to Gitesi. *"I was running with my father when we ran into a group of militia. He was killed, but one of the soldiers knew him and decided to take me to his house in Kibuye to work for him as a servant. In Kibuye, he told his leader that I was his niece and after a few days he told me to leave his house and run away in the night. I ran through the forest and came to the Bisesero area.*

"The man who helped me is not in prison yet because no one has reported him to the police, but if there is no one who saw him killing people, I don't think he should be punished. I am just thankful that he saved my life that day instead of killing me. I think he would have saved my father if he was alone, but because he was in a group of militia it was impossible because they would have seen him as a traitor.

"I was so happy to be with other children when I came to the JAM Orphanage in 1994. We became like brothers and sisters and we comforted each other when one of us was sad. I still have many friends from the orphanage and I am so happy to meet them around the area I now live. I still call them my brothers and sisters."

When Speciose left the JAM Orphanage she was in primary six. Her uncle came to work in the orphanage and encouraged her to leave in order for her to become accustomed to the way of living outside. *"I was scared to meet people outside and did not want to leave the children in the orphanage. When I left JAM I started thinking about what happened in the war and I thought that I might get killed when I came outside. However, when I met people I discovered that they had changed and they have good hearts."*

Speciose Mukakarisa
Age 21
Born in Gitesi.
Region: Bisesero, Kibuye.
Attends Groupe Scolere Indangabures in
Ruhango, secondary level 4.

Surviving the bloodbath

Olive attends a boarding school in Gitarama and is happy there, as she is able to concentrate on her studies. She has dreams of becoming a lawyer, so as to work with human rights. Those that know Olive describe her as a very happy girl no matter what problems she faces. However, when asked to tell us about her experience of the war, a dark veil falls over her eyes and she begins her story:

"We had to run from our home the day the war started and were stopped by militia. My parents were the ones they wanted and were murdered right there. My sister and I managed to escape, but were soon separated. I followed a group of strangers to take cover in the bush. We were discovered by the attackers, who proceeded to murder all the men in the group. Children were taken and thrown into a deep ditch. In the evening we managed to climb out and make our way to a cave in the mountains where we came across other refugees. We stayed there for five days until again we were discovered by militia. They began a bloodbath, killing many. My leg was injured with a spear but I managed to escape. When night fell, I was able to leave, not knowing where to go.

"An elderly lady took me home to her house where she offered me food and water. I was unable to eat. I was exhausted and my stomach hurt terribly. It was not long after that, that the lady's sons returned home. They ordered their mother to send me away. They were involved in the killings that had been going on and did not want me in their house. The lady told me to run as her sons would kill me. I fled, not knowing where to go or hide. Exhausted, I came across a small river filled with blood. This scared me, for I realised that militia may still be in the vicinity. I changed my direction and eventually caught up with some people on the road, trying to make their way to one of the refugee camps. At this stage I was feeling very ill, suffering from worms, scabies, skin diseases, hunger and malaria. I believe that these symptoms were caused by drinking dirty water and eating raw food. I believed I would die before the war was over and I felt that it was better to die than to continue suffering.

"We finally reached a refugee camp where I was reunited with my older brother and uncle. Weeks later, the militia surrounded our camp with many traditional weapons. Suddenly there was a burst of gunfire and I was certain I was going to die soon. To our relief, we saw the militia scatter and were confronted by the RPA who were there to save us. My brother and I were taken to an orphanage in Byimana where we were reunited with my younger sister. I was so happy as I thought she had not survived the war.

"We spent five years in the orphanage and, although we were taken care of, I longed to be part of a family again and my uncle eventually was able to put me into a boarding school. During the holidays, he rents a house where we can stay. We don't have much money, as my uncle looks after all of us and we don't get any aid from anyone. We are struggling but we stay patient, believing that God will provide for us."

Olive Mukandahiro
Age 16
Born in Gitarama.
Lives with her uncle, Alexis Muvara,
Kigali City.
Attends Saint Joseph Boarding School
in Kapgai, secondary level 4.

Aimee Mukeshimana
Age 16
Born in Ruhango village.
Region: Saint Jean College, Nyarusange.
Attends S1 at Saint Jean College,
Secondary School, Gitarama.

Hoping for a job in radio or television

Aimee attends a college just outside Gitarama along with four of her friends from the JAM Orphanage. She loves to study and her biggest wish is for someone to sponsor her studies and materials. She worries that she may need to forsake her studies to work, in order to keep the rest of her family alive and well. When asked what career she would like to pursue, Aimee says she would like to be a nurse or teacher, only because these careers are most available. When asked what she would really like to do, she smiles, **"I would prefer to get a job where I can work with literature. I would love to get a job inside television or radio."**

Aimee's experiences of the war differed from most children and she and her family were very fortunate in comparison to others. She lived with both her parents until 1990 when her father died due to illness. He was employed in a high position and was able to provide for his family's every need. When the war finally broke out in 1994, militia stormed into their house, removed all their belongings and informed the children they were going to kill their mother. They made her sit in a chair and took the baby she was holding. Suddenly they changed their minds and said that their mother would die some time during the war anyway, so they would leave her alone. Aimee truly believes that God was their protector that night. Although Aimee recognised the perpetrators as people from her village, the family decided to stay at home until June 1994. The situation became far too dangerous and they decided to flee later that month. They made their way to another district, where they were confronted and their lives once again threatened. Aimee's mother convinced the attackers to allow them to go back to their village so that they could die at home. On returning to their village, Aimee and her family discovered that the Rwandan Patriotic Army had taken control and they were safe.

Life began to normalise when suddenly, in 1997, her mother died. It was discovered that Aimee's mother had been poisoned by a woman living in their village. She knew who the woman was, but says she does not feel hatred towards her and in her words: **"It happened and it was finished. I have forgiven her.**

"After the death of my mother, my two brothers and I stayed with our oldest sister. However, she could not afford to cover all our needs and therefore decided to go to the Ministry of Social Affairs to ask for help. They decided to send the three of us to an orphanage and at the end of 1997 we came to the JAM Orphanage in Gitarama. The orphanage has taken good care of us. They treat us as their children and they never leave us alone. By loving us they help us forget what happened to us in the war."

Taking care of each other

"Up to December last year I was living in an orphanage in Kibuye, but now I am waiting for IRC to finish a house for me and I will start living my own life."

Assiel says that it will be a challenge, because it will be the first time he has ever lived alone, looking after himself.

"I stayed one year at the JAM Fred Nkunda Orphanage (1994 to 1995) I got everything that I needed in the orphanage and I was very thankful and happy to go to the orphanage because I did not have anywhere to go after the war. I still have many good friends from the JAM Orphanage that I play together with today. We are like a family and even now I stay with some friends from JAM who had to leave Kibuye Orphanage with me. We take care of each other."

Assiel says that he did not choose to be alone after the war. If he could find any family who survived the war, he would want to go and stay with them. He feels that it is important to live with a family, although very often distant relatives can mistreat orphans because they don't care for them as their own.

Assiel finds it is difficult to forget about the war because many innocent people were killed.

"My family were killed in the beginning of the war, and I had to manage on my own. I was very sad and afraid when I was left alone. One day in the middle of the war some killers threw a spear towards the group and it hit me in my stomach. I fell down and lay still. The soldiers believed that I had died and left me alone. I also thought that I was going to die because I was bleeding so much. I realised that the war was over when I was taken to Goma in the DRC, where I was treated in a hospital. I was happy that the war was over but I could not imagine what my life would be like without my parents.

"I was glad to go to the orphanage where they gave me new clothes to wear. I met many other children of my own age to play with and I was very happy there.

"I like my country, but sometimes the people who live here are not good persons. If they were good, the genocide would never even have happened. When people meet, they appear friendly and everything on the outside looks good, but one doesn't know what is hidden in people's hearts.

"I want the Rwandan people to know that we all have the same blood and that we share everything. God created all people in his image and we should act according to this."

Assiel Munyakarama
Age 18
Born in Kibuye.
Region: Gitabura, Kibuye.
Attends Esapan Secondary School, level 2.

"*Fred Nkunda loved people so much*"

"I live with my 26-year-old cousin in Mubuga, close to the market. There is also a playing ground for soccer. I watch Rwandan television or video at a neighbour's house. I don't have a problem with my life. I like to watch movies, to play volleyball, football and billiards. I like karate and Jackie Chan movies.

"My cousin is a farmer. When I was living in the orphanage, he saw that I needed to go out and took me in so that I can also start with life outside the orphanage. It is normally not good to stay in the place where you were not born, because people can sometimes say that you should go back to your home.

"I went to JAM in 1995, just after the war. The life there was good and I remember the director, Fred. I heard that Fred died before he could come to visit us. We were very sad to hear that Fred died. Some children even went to Gitarama for the funeral. He was a very good man. I haven't seen anybody that can compare to him. He loved people so much.

"At the moment I would like to go ahead with my secondary studies, so that I can help myself in the future. When I am finished, I would like to have a big garage of my own where I can manage the staff who are working in my garage. I really want to learn to be a mechanic.

"When the war broke out we didn't know what was happening exactly. One Friday, all the militia from Gitarama and all the different areas came to Muhira area. They surrounded all of us and opened fire. I was injured in the back by a grenade. At that time my mother had already died, but my father was still alive and tried to wash the wound where I was hit. In the mornings he took me to the bushes to hide me. He left me food in the bush to eat. In the evenings he came to pick me up and take me home. I knew that I could die after some time, but God kept helping me until I was healed.

"Throughout the war I moved around with my father. He died around 1 pm on the day that at around 3 pm the French came into the area. I am sad when I think that he died just two hours before the French came. After his death, my older brother started to care for me like my father was doing. I have two brothers, one in Kigali and one in school in Ngoma. They cleaned my wounds until I was healed. My brother in Kigali is a driver and he is supporting me.

"Most of the people who killed my family died from illnesses in prison. I used to go back to where I was born and I asked their relatives how they were doing. Everybody just wants peace. It made me sad that they died without me being able to meet them and ask them why they did what they did. If they could ask me forgiveness for what they had done, I could have forgiven them... I have forgiven them in any case. I just wish for peace and a good life. That's all."

Claver Ngendahimana
Age 18
Born in Nyarutovu.
Region: Mubuga, Rusenyi, Kibuye.
Attends P6 in Mubuga Primary School.
Brother is head boy of ESI in Ngoma.

"Many people find it difficult to forgive"

Bernard works as an assistant in the taxi buses. He started helping the taxi drivers when he finished primary school. He helps people in and out of the bus and only earns a tip when the bus is full. He hopes one day to learn how to drive a bus of his own. So far the driver he works with has taught him how to drive a normal car so he wants to get a driving permit so that he can also become a taxi driver one day.

"I came to JAM in 1997 and left the orphanage in 2001 because the Government wanted me to be close to my place of origin. I don't have any relatives left in Kibuye, but I have one relative in Gisenyi. I don't want to go and stay with him because he does not have means to care for me. I would rather stay here with my friends in Kibuye.

"Before the war I stayed with my brother and my parents. We had a good life and we were farmers in Kibuye.

"When the war broke out my father was killed and I continued to hide with my mother and big brother. Later they were also killed. The militia beat me with sticks until I fell down and they believed I was dead. I woke up later and hid in bushes near our destroyed house until the war was over. Near the end of the war some RPA soldiers brought me to Gitarama where I was sent to the JAM Orphanage.

Bernard Nshimiyimana
Age 16
Born in Kibuye.
Region: Kibuye ville, Rubengera.
Attends primary school in Kibuye, level 6.

"I watched so many people being killed by the militia in the war. They were killed in different ways. Many people were thrown in the lake or down toilet pits. Some people were even buried in the ground while they were still alive.

"I don't think I can ever forget about the terrible things that happened in 1994. When I cook or go to sleep in the evenings I start thinking about my family and I feel very lonely.

"I have forgiven the people who were involved in the genocide. I think that reconciliation only will be possible between a few people, because many people find it difficult to forgive.

"I think the cause of the war was bad leadership. It was not the local people who started the war, but the leaders. I don't know if the war will ever happen again because the people who were forced by leaders to kill have regretted and they don't want to be involved in something like the genocide again.

"I think it is important that the world realises what happened in the genocide. The people who lived through the war must never forget what happened in order to prevent it from happening again."

"When I forgive, I forgive from my heart"

"I am in school now, but before going back to school I was living in the JAM Fred Nkunda Orphanage. I started in P1 when I was still at JAM. When I left that place, we started to lead a bad life.

"I left the JAM Orphanage in February 1996. When I arrived here, I didn't find any relatives and the tracing organisation put me with a neighbour who was renting a house from someone. The neighbour went to Kigali alone and never came back. After two months I saw that he was not coming back and my life was becoming worse. I went to stay with another neighbour. If I see him again, I would ask him if he went because of shortage of food or if he didn't like me. I still don't know why he went.

Zacharie Rutijana
Age 19
Born in Ryarutambara.
Region: Ngoma, Kibuye.
Currently in P6 in Ngoma Primary School

"I spent one year without going to school, and because I didn't have a family I lost hope for the future. I kept thinking how I could go back to JAM Orphanage. I even thought of walking from Kibuye to Gitarama because I didn't have money for transport. I heard that some of the children that I was living with went to an orphanage in Kibuye. I went to talk to the manager of the orphanage, and I went back to school in 1997. I started again in P2 and currently I am in P6.

"I would like to go back to my place of origin, to the land of my parents, to build a small house to live in. I can look for a child to be with me who also has the same problems so that we can be company for one another. If I go to school he can stay at home.

"Now I am planning to finish P6. In my area there are only three families – all the other families died. On weekends or during the holidays I will spend one day working on the land so that I can get something to eat. If there was something else to do, I would do it, but I have to start with the thing that gives me food.

"If you study, it is difficult if you don't find notebooks and always have to borrow pens and notebooks. As you can see it is a big problem. When you see somebody who is educated, he doesn't face many problems, because he can fend for himself, wherever he goes.

"The problem today is when you, as an orphan, see other children who have families, and you see how they live, it makes you think that you were also born like them and could have had a good life like theirs.

"I don't have a problem with the people who killed my family. If somebody can come to me and say from his heart, 'I am the one who did this to you – this is why you have this bad life, I want you to forgive me...' I can forgive him. When I forgive, I forgive from my heart, because I want the relationships between people to be as they were before."

"*I will not talk to my children about the Genocide*"

"When I came back to Bisesero I was poor and there was nothing to start with. There was no foundation. Since that time I have just been trying to survive. I have built my house in the same place where we stayed before. I farm coffee, sweet potatoes, beans and cassava, but we don't get a very good harvest. The animals we had were eaten during the war, so there are no animals to farm either. Even this house was given to me by an organisation. You can only get money if you work and dig up somebody else's land. If, for example, you or your child falls sick, they charge you 50,000 or 60,000 francs. I will probably have to sell the corrugated steel roof of my house in an emergency. You have a problem if you don't have somebody like a family who can support you or give you some means.

"When the war started we were eight people in the family. We all ran away. They destroyed our houses and took our animals. They ate the cows that we had. They also beat me, so I am not strong either. All my relatives and my surrounding relatives were killed until I was the only one left of my whole family in the area. When I thought about the people who were committing the murders, I thought that were sent by the devil to kill people.

"The war went on every day for about four months, until the French troops arrived in the area. They only found 500 people out of 80,000 who were here before the killings. If you visit the memorial, you can see how many people died. I estimate that around 500,000 people died in the area of Kibuye. Many people were thrown in ditches and bushes and, when we ran, we were jumping over bodies. The whole area was littered with bodies. It was just a miracle of God that some of us survived.

"When I left the orphanage I came here and decided to marry at a young age. The name of my first born is Uwineza Claudine and the youngest is Uwase Beatrice. I will not talk to my children about the genocide, so that they won't grow up with a bad heart. Maybe they will come to understand it elsewhere because they will grow up without neighbours and they will see the destroyed things around them.

"If the Government keeps teaching reconciliation and unity, it will reach an end and if the judges do a good job to punish those who committed the crimes, Rwandans will come together. My children will know about the genocide, because it is a crime that doesn't get old. When a child like mine, who was born after the war, goes to the memorial they will see that their families lost lives, so of course they will know what happened.

"When I think about all these things I plan for the future. Because of poverty I plan, but I don't reach the goals... If I get means I want my children to grow up and have a good life, to go to school and get knowledge. I don't need them to be like me who never went to school because of the bad former Government.

"If I had cows, the children would at least have milk to drink, but of course it cannot be the same as before. Before I lost my family we had many cows — around ten. We also had ten goats and banana plantations. All those banana trees were cut down. The land has become unfertilised because of a lack of fertiliser from animals. This is why, if you try to grow something, you don't produce what you were producing before. So the poverty just increases, because you don't have a foundation."

Casimir Ruzindana
Age 22
Born in 1980 in Karama, Musenyi, Kibuye.
Completed P3.

"We must share what we have"

Fleur's exact age is not known as she was just a baby, about two years old, when she was found in a terrible condition, lying in some bushes during 1994. It is believed that her parents abandoned her in the hope that she would survive, as they knew that they would probably not. Soldiers from the UN immediately took little Fleur to the JAM Fred Nkunda Orphanage where they began nourishing her back to health.

Fleur now lives with her foster mother Ndihano, who tells the story of Fleur:

"My two daughters were separated from me during the war and were placed in the JAM Orphanage. They were asked to help take care of baby Fleur, because they were older than most of the other girls. Once they were reunited with me, they told me all about this little girl, and I made the decision to adopt her. I approached the orphanage and they agreed. Fleur is a beautiful little girl and I love her like my own child and take care of her like I did with my older daughters. I did not tell Fleur that she was not my own daughter until early this year. I did not want her to feel different. She was very unhappy when I told her, but even before I told her, she occasionally became sad and unhappy and started crying. She had bad dreams and remembered things from the war. Because she was maturing, I wanted her to know about her past and that she had other parents when she was a little baby.

"My biggest wish is to see Fleur grow up into a beautiful lady before I die. I have started having heart problems, but I pray that I will live to see her happily married.

Fleur added: *"When I finish primary school I want to go to secondary school to study French and Mathematics. I would like to become a Mathematics teacher; it should be easy to teach other children Mathematics because I like it so much. Education is important for children because one day they will grow up and work for their country.*

"When I come home from school I help my mother clean the house and I often look after the small children when my sisters are around. When I don't have to help in the house, I play ball with my friends in the neighbourhood."

Fleur's mother wishes that every Rwandan family would understand the importance of taking care of orphans. *"We must share what we have. I hope that families in this country will take responsibility for the children who lost their parents in the genocide."*

Fleur Uwimana
Age 11
Region: Gitarama ville.
Attends URG Primary School, level 5.

"It is not easy for victims to forgive, but it is necessary"

These last few years of living in the orphanage, Marcel dreams about living an independent life, but he does not have any place to stay or any means to provide for himself.

"From 1994 up to now, I've never been out of the orphanages," he says. *"In 1996 I was moved from JAM Orphanage to Kibuye to be close to my place of origin. I was cared for in the orphanage and they helped me to study. But to live in an orphanage all your childhood is not good for a child because one needs to be used to staying in a family and be integrated in society.*

"Before the war I had both parents and I had no problems, but when the war started I did not understand what was happening because I had never experienced a war before. I just heard that my family said that people were being killed so we had to run. In the nights people were sleeping either in the forests or in broken houses. My father and I slept in a destroyed house in the evenings and he went to look for some vegetables for us to eat. My mother was killed in the beginning of the war. My father found her body and buried her. My father and I were hiding in bushes close to each other. Suddenly I heard a man shouting, but I stayed in my bush until I thought it was safe to come out. I went over to where my father was hiding and found his body. The next morning some other people helped me to bury my father."

Marcel doesn't know why the genocide happened and doesn't want to think much about it either. He says that he never talks about the war because it's not good to talk about it. He feels that the only times people should talk about it, is to try and find ways to prevent the war from happening again.

"I think that many of the killers have regretted what they did. Some of them have even publicly confessed and asked for forgiveness. I don't think it is easy for the victims to forgive, but it is necessary if we want to prevent it from happening again. God has been helping me all my life. He protected me in the war and He was the One who stopped the war. I hope that God will help me to find a place to live and give me means to continue my studies. I also wish that my country will have peace in the future and that there will never be another war in Rwanda."

Marcel Bayingana
Age 21
Born in Karama.
Region: Musenyi, Kibuye.
Attends ESIM Secondary School, level 5.

"*Sponsorship is necessary*"

"In the holidays I used to go to the garage asking them to teach me about cars and how to repair cars. However this holiday, I went to JAM Orphanage because I had heard that they had started computer training for the orphans. I spent all day there and sometimes I slept over in the orphanage as well, because it is very important to learn how to use the computer to be able to get a good job."

Jean Bosco often stays with his soldier friends in Gitarama. He is not too happy or secure staying with an unfamiliar family as he feels that they may treat him badly or even kill him one day. He feels at ease when staying with the soldiers because they have experienced war just as he has, and feels that there is greater understanding between them all.

"My life after the war was very bad, but day by day it got better. When I was in the orphanage JAM paid my school fees, but now I have to pay for my own studies without any help and I don't know if I will manage to finish school. The only thing I know is that if I am not able to finish my studies I will join the army and become a soldier."

Jean Bosco did not want to share his experiences of the war with us, as he felt it was private between himself and his family members. He does however feel that it is necessary for the rest of the world to come to a realisation of what happened to Rwanda during the genocide.

"When I was in the orphanage the children often told visitors about what happened to them in the war and the visitors felt sorry for them and decided to help them or sponsor them to go to school. When you have no family to take care of you, it is very necessary to get someone to sponsor you. Some of the children who are sponsored from people abroad are now very happy and have good lives."

Despite Jean Bosco's unfulfilled wishes, he says that he is fortunate to have his sisters and one brother alive and well with him today. His brother is a soldier in the DRC and his two sisters live at the JAM Orphanage.

"I am very thankful because I know that many orphans don't have any family at all and that must be terrible..."

Jean Bosco Bizimana
Age 17
Born in Satinsyi.
Region: Gisenyi.
Attends S3 in College St Emmanuel in
Hanuka. Was in JAM 1996-1999.

Working hard for a better future

Vianney came to Kigali in 1995 with his aunt. He later moved out and now stays in a house with some of his friends. A friend arranged a good job for him in a nearby hotel. He feels that his life now is quite good because he has the money to buy the necessary food and many other things he needs from month to month.

He is not interested in going back to his place of origin because everything was destroyed in the war, hence the reason he now prefers to stay in the city. Like most other orphans, he wishes to acquire a "good life" of his own, with a family and home and enough clothes and food to eat each day. He desires to earn enough money to pay the rent for his house and to buy small gifts for his sister who also survived the genocide.

Besides his sister, Vianney has a cousin in the United States and a few cousins in Canada that left Rwanda before the 1994 genocide occurred.

"My cousins grew up there because their parents ran away in 1954 and 1979. They don't understand what happened to us in 1994. I don't know what has happened to them or if they still feel Rwandan, but I hope that they will come back one day because their mother still lives in Uganda. Sometimes I think that if my parents had gone with them I would still have my parents and we would be happy, because a child who has parents can ask for nice clothes and things, but an orphan does not know how to get these things.

"Many families that take orphans in and promise to give them good lives start mistreating them when they arrive in their homes. I think that they want to help the orphans initially, but their hearts change when the orphans don't behave as the parents would like them to. I think that this happens as a result of the war, because the orphans get traumatized or depressed when thinking about the war and the families don't know how to help them or to treat them in the right way. If I compare my life with other orphans, I think that I have been lucky to have better living conditions than many of them."

He believes that many people want reconciliation to take place in Rwanda but they struggle to forget about the war and put it in their past. Reconciliation is a slow and painful process and he believes that if the victims know that the killers are being punished for what they did, it might be easier for everybody to wish for reconciliation and start working towards it.

Vianney Jean Marie Bugingo
Age about 23
Born in Ntyazo, Butare.
Finished secondary school in level 4.

Still difficult to concentrate because of the war

"When the war started we had to leave our place of origin and run to Bisesero. We were running around hiding in bushes, until my family were killed. I kept moving around with my father's cousin until the war ended.

"Apart from my father and one brother, I saw all the other family members being killed. My family were chopped to death with pangas. When the war started we decided to separate and hide in different places. I was with my mother, grandmother and sisters. We reached a place where we could drink water. My grandmother and I kept going while my mother and sisters stayed behind. A soldier ran towards the group of women which my mother and sisters were in and killed them all. My grandmother and I ran away crying.

"I stayed with my grandmother until she was also killed. While I was watching from another bush they dragged her out and killed her. I was very young in the war and I did not know how to protect myself. Miraculously I was not even hit or hurt in any way during the war. It was only God who protected me from the militia.

"French soldiers asked us if we wanted to stay with RP soldiers, or if we wanted them to take us to a place near the border of Congo. We went to the RP soldiers and they brought us to the JAM Fred Nkunda Orphanage in Kapgai. The staff investigated and managed to find my place of origin. My relatives in Bisesero came and picked me up and took me to my father's cousin. He is a good man, who tries his best to give me a future.

"Sometimes I think about my parents, but I try to forget it by singing or drawing. It distracts me and it helps me to forget. If I keep thinking about what happened I can't concentrate on anything and it is very difficult to study."

Emmanuel Harerimana
Age 14
Born in Gitwa.
Region: Bisesero.
Attends Esapan Secondary School, Kibuye.

Overcoming crippling difficulties

Emmanuel was born with deformed legs. His parents died when he was nine years old so he lived with his aunt, uncle and their seven children in Gitarama. When the war began, Emmanuel and his aunt fled from their home with him in a bag tied onto her back. They ran to the mountains and hid in bushes and derelict homes where they survived on almost nothing for many weeks.

Emmanuel says, **"I remember that my aunt took me on her back and carried me everyday. When the militia came, trying to get us, my aunt never left me. She always protected me and was with me everyday for the three months of the war."**

This family was fortunate as they all survived the war and returned to Gitarama. Emmanuel's uncle was referred by their pastor to a programme for handicapped children in one of the orphanages, and so Emmanuel found himself at the Fred Nkunda Life Centre.

He moved to an orphanage in Kibuye for further training and development and unfortunately lost contact with his family in Gitarama.

Later he returned to the Fred Nkunda Life Centre where the staff started to search for his family. He was sent to Gatagara Orthopaedic Hospital where he underwent surgery for his badly curved legs. Emmanuel was given braces and crutches and he slowly started to learn to walk.

His aunt had lost hope of seeing him ever again, but in December 2000 she heard two men talking outside her house, mentioning Emmanuel's name.

The man was looking for Emmanuel's family. His aunt was so happy and could almost not believe that her little Emmanuel was coming home at last. Emmanuel returned home in February 2001, still walking on a pair of crutches and supporting braces on his legs. His condition has improved to such an extent that he can even stand for short periods without the aid of his crutches.

Emmanuel is so glad to be back 'home' and brings much joy to the family. He loves to play with the younger children and often spends time after school helping his aunt prepare dinner for all.

Emmanuel Iyamuremye
Age 15
Region: Gitarama ville.
Attends Gahogo Primary School.

Married in the orphanage

John and Irene struggled through much hardship during the Genocide, but today they are happily married and proud parents of three boys, Cyuzuzo who is six years old, Patrick five and Rene two.

John explains *"I have a good life. I am married; I have three beautiful children and a job that enables me to pay the school fees for relatives who I am responsible for. It is a challenge for me to have all these children under my care, but I trust in God and know that He will provide for me and my family as long as I live."*

John and Irene's main goal is to ensure that their children receive a good education, enabling them to become more and more independent as they grow older. They both know the value of gaining the best knowledge and skills and so strive towards this goal each day. What they mostly want for their children is to know God as they grow up. John would really like his wife and children to come and live with him in Gitarama where he works, but it is impossible because they need to keep the land in Kibuye to produce their food to eat. Fortunately John is able to keep his oldest son with him as he attends primary school in Gitarama.

John, a supervisor at JAM, is thankful for the job God blessed him with. He says that he came to the orphanage (then called Abundant Life International) when Fred was running it all on his own. *"I am so grateful that I could stay in the orphanage even though I was older than the other children."*

At the orphanage, John was responsible for cooking and teaching the children worship songs. The manager promoted him to supervisor and to this day he continues to share his faith with the children.

"When JAM took over the running of the orphanage, I was employed as a supervisor above the other workers. It was during this time that I confided in Fred, the orphanage manager, that I wanted to get married. He gave us his blessings and we got married in the orphanage on 18 February 1995 with all the orphans as spectators."

John loves to preach. *"Wherever I go I talk to people about Jesus."* People in the village respect John and often ask for his advice.

Irene was born in Birambo village in Kibuye. When the war started her father and five of her sisters and brothers were killed. She did not witness the murders, but she heard that the militia hacked them to death. Irene and her younger sister were the only survivors. When the war was over the RPA soldiers told villagers that they could return to their homes. Irene was taken to the orphanage in Gitarama.

John shared his war experience: *"When the war started I was working during the day and in the evenings. I went to pray with my friends or visit hospitals to hand out food to patients and poor people. I knew that the war would come when we heard on the radio that the President had been killed. We also noticed that people were starting to distrust each other. There were many people from the Tutsi tribe living in Kibuye, so the city became a target area for the militia. They killed our families, burned our houses and stole our cows."*

Tragedy finally struck one day while John and his mother were praying with other Christians. They heard gunshots and saw soldiers coming. *"We had to run away in different directions. My mother couldn't get away fast enough and was discovered by the militia. They hacked her to death with a panga.*

"In July the French troops came to save us. They asked us to join the army, which I did. At that stage of the war I was tired of fighting and decided to defect. I went to the Catholic Centre in Kapgai where I met Fred. He asked me to help him look for children who did not have any place to stay, and I started working for him.

"If a person lost all of his family in the war it is difficult for him to forgive. But things are looking better. People live together in spite of the past. The Government teaches people to understand each other. I see that people intermarry and they are slowly but surely starting to socialise. They have started to interact."

John believes that God has worked through JAM International to reach lost children in Rwanda. *"If it was not for JAM I don't know what my life would have been today. Many of the orphans who have been helped by JAM can actually thank this organisation for saving their lives. JAM has become like a mother for many of these children."*

John Basomingera
Age 35
Born in Bisesero, Kibuye.
Works as a supervisor at the JAM Orphanage.

Irene Mutawiyera
Age 28.
Born in Birambo.
Works at home, digging the land and looking after their children.

Unemployed – through lack of education

Emmanuel is currently unemployed. He rents a house in Kibuye town, but can't pay his rent at the moment and is not sure how much longer the landlord will allow him to stay in the house.

Emmanuel had many narrow escapes during the genocide. He escaped militia suspicion for a month by being a herd boy for a Hutu lady who knew his father before the war began. She protected him from her own sons who were involved in the genocide until she was reported to the Governor, who ordered her sons to kill Emmanuel. The lady reluctantly asked Emmanuel to leave. He later sneaked back to her home because he was very ill with malaria. He longed for the warmth of the fire in the kitchen instead of the cold Rwandan rain outside. However one of the lady's sons discovered him there and fetched a stick to kill Emmanuel, so he fled immediately.

Emmanuel was eventually captured by the militia after a bitter neighbour guided him into their hands pretending to direct him to the French troops. Happily, only a few hours later they told him that the war was over and there was no use in killing him.

After amazing escapes time and time again, he was taken to Gitarama where he met Fred Nkunda and another Ugandan. They were looking for orphans to take to an establishment known today as Fred Nkunda Life Centre. After a short time in another orphanage Emmanuel dropped out of school because of his age and bad results.

Today his hope rests in studying in a technical field so that he can maybe get a job as a mechanic and get a place of his own place to stay.

"When I see how my friends have succeeded I understand that education is very important to get a good job. Education makes people bright and open-minded. But I don't have enough money to pay for my studies, so my first priority is to get a job to pay for my studies. I try my best to get something to eat every day, but it is difficult when you have neither money nor land to grow vegetables."

Emmanuel Kanamugire
Age 23
Born in Murangara, Kibuye.
Finished school in primary 5.

Reconciliation and unity – the way forward

Innocent stays with his older brother, wife and child in Bisesero, situated far up in the mountains of Kibuye. He came to stay with them after he left the orphanage in Gitarama.

"My mother, my two younger brothers and my older brother were killed by a group of militia on 13th May. I was running with two of my brothers, my sister and my father in the following weeks. After a few days both my father and brother were killed.

"One morning when we were going from our house up to Bisesero we were surrounded by the militia. While we ran to escape from the soldiers I was shot in my arm and I fell down. I was unconscious but woke up some minutes later and managed to move to another place. A group of soldiers found me there and they hit me on my head and I fell down as if dead.

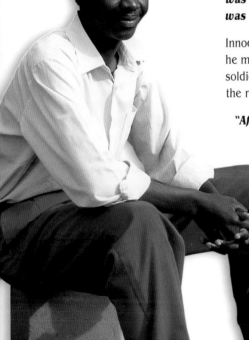

Innocent Karogora
Age 20
Born in Kibuye.
Region: Nyanitovu, Bisesero.
Attends ESIM Secondary School, level 2.

"I lay there until the evening when the militia went home. I prayed to God to protect me but I believed that my last hour had come. I was bleeding all over and I was so very tired and would just sleep. After a while my mind was clearer and I managed to crawl close to a path on the side of me. A man who was passing by discovered me and offered to help me. On the way to our house we saw my brother on the other side of the valley and he came to help carry me. I was happy to be alive, but thinking about my family who had all been killed I was also ready to die."

Innocent was taken to Goma in the DRC for medical help. When he came back to Rwanda he met his brother and sister who had walked 70 km from Kibuye to Gitarama with RPA soldiers. His brother then took him to an orphanage because of the bad conditions in the refugee camp.

"After a while we went back to our own piece of land where my brother started working on the land. Only the walls of our house were left. We asked some neighbours to give us some old roof sheets to cover our house. Later an NGO helped us with new tin sheets for the roof.

"Today I know that one tribe wanted to eliminate another one. I can't say that we should revenge what the killers did to us, but I think that they should be punished according to the law. I think that the situation can be better in the future if the Government continues to teach reconciliation and unity among the Rwandan people, but I don't think that the genocide of 1994 will ever be forgotten. Even though I had not experienced the war of 1959 I still hear about it. In the same way I think my children will still hear about the war in 1994 when they grow up and will tell their children."

Sole breadwinner for the family

Beata is the oldest sister in the family and is responsible for her younger sisters, Vestine, aged 20, Jaqueline who is 18 years, Nyiraminana, 11 years and her brother Nyandwi who is 16 years old. Beata was with her younger sisters during the war and they were all brought to the orphanage once the war was over.

"I am struggling because I have to take care of my younger sisters and brother. It is my responsibility to give them food, clothes and whatever they need while my only job at the moment is to buy food in different markets and to then sell it in the local market in Gitarama."

They are all very content and happy staying with one another, and appreciate having each other as brothers and sisters after the war. The only problems they face as a family is lack of food during the months she makes little money. Her youngest sister is the only one attending school as Beata is the sole breadwinner who brings in an income every month. The other brothers and sisters stay at home to work on the land. Beata had to stop school in 1994 as she fell very sick, and was unable to continue.

Beata Karugwera
Age 21
Region: Ville de Gitarama.
Completed only primary 2 in 1994 because of illness.

"I went to the doctor and he told me that I had stomach problems. When it is very stressful in my job, I get sick and have breathing problems. I don't know if it was the war that made me fall sick or if it was the bad conditions we lived in after the war. When I fall sick, I think my mother would have cared for me and taken me to the doctor if she were alive."

Beata and her brothers and sisters survived the war by hiding in banana trees, bushes and ditches, fearful of death all the time. They fled through the Rwandan countryside until they found safety with troops from the advancing RPA.

"After the war I asked myself why the genocide happened. I heard that people were coming to kill the Tutsi tribe. I did not understand what motives they had but, when the war was over, Rwanda was like an empty country. People who survived the war started asking why they were the lucky ones who were not killed. However today people seem to be recovering and they live together in peace."

Beata hopes that her health will improve and that her family will be able to live a good life in the future. She feels that genocide might occur again because she believes that some people have not changed their attitude after the war.

"Some people are still angry with others and might not be very happy about all the people who survived the war."

Fending for himself

Juvenal is an independent young man trying to create a foundation for his future. He doesn't live with a family and has to fend for himself. During the holidays the school places him with different families. The genocide fund assists him with school fees but he still needs to buy his own notebooks and pens. Juvenal's education is very important to him. He will finish secondary school next year and dreams of going to university if the Government can support him. He also wants to study computers in Kibuye and Kigali.

Before the war life was carefree. Juvenal was part of a family of eight children and his parents were farmers. When the war broke out they went into hiding at the Catholic cathedral. The militia came and he hid in the mountains and forests in the Kibuye area until the militia eventually caught him.

Juvenal Kayishema
Age 21
Born in Kibuye.
Region: Ruyenzi, Burunga, Kibuye.
Attends Esapan Secondary School, level 6.

"They took me with them. On the way I met my brother and sister whom the militia had taken to kill. The soldiers beat us with sticks and spears and my sister and brother died immediately. I managed to crawl into a bush nearby. I didn't see my mother and father being killed, but people told me. I was very sad but did not expect to survive either."

French soldiers took him to the RP soldiers who brought him to the JAM Fred Nkunda Orphanage. *"I wished that I had been killed but I started secondary school and felt that life was getting better. I met children who had experienced the war as well and we comforted each other. When I was old enough, I left the orphanage and went to Kigali to look for my uncle. He helped me and encouraged me to start school.*

"I cannot predict my future. It is up to God to make my life better. But I don't think I can ever be as happy as I was when I was living with my parents. I want to show Rwandan people the consequences of what was done in the war. I can't see that people have any benefit of killing their fellow countrymen. I believe in God because He has done much for me. He protected me during the war. I thank God for organisations like JAM, because they help people who have needs.

"Because of the problems I went through in the war I would like to help other people in need, especially the orphans because they suffered so much in the war."

"My parents' land has bad memories for me"

Evode now lives in a rural area in Gitarama, together with his uncle, step-aunt and three cousins. One of Evode's two sisters was with him in the orphanage before they were separated and fostered to different families. Evode is like many children, prevented from going to school, often because their help around the home and in the fields is seen to be far more important than school and many families cannot afford the fees for educating their children.

"I am happy in the family. The only problem is I can't go to school. I would like to become a mechanic because I like to fix cars and it would be nice to work in a garage. At home I have to go and fetch water every morning. The rest of the day I look after animals and I work on the land together with my cousins. When I have finished my duties at home, I play soccer with my friends in the village."

Evode was born in Mushibata outside Gitarama. He stayed together with his parents, four brothers and sisters. *"My parents were farmers and we had our own cows and we had vegetables on our land."*

"I still have the land that we lived on before the war, but I don't like to go back there because of all the memories. We don't know any people there and there are no relatives staying in the area either.

When the war started I remember that the militia came to our village. We all ran away from our house and were separated. But I remember that some soldiers found my mother and my cousin and killed them. After their death I ran away but I did not know where to go. I tried to find a place where I could hide.

"I was very afraid though because the militia found where the people were hiding, dragged them out and killed them.

"During the war I was running around in the mountains. Sometimes I hid in ditches while other times I hid in bushes. I can't remember what I ate or how I slept. I just remember that I was running from place to place until the war was over."

Evode Kimenyi
Age 15
Born in Mushibata.
Region: Gitarama Rural.

Dreaming of building a house on his father's land

Vianney lives with his uncle, aunt and grandmother in Bisesero. He struggles to buy food daily and rents out his father's land to assist with the daily costs of living. During the holidays he doesn't get much chance to do the things other children do as he has to tend to his uncle's cows. He feels that he's been treated unfairly by his uncle because he keeps his money that he earns from renting out his father's land. *"When my aunt and uncle get hold of my money they use it on themselves. They have two girls and one boy who are younger than I am. They treat me differently from their own children."*

Vianney is happiest when he's at school with his friends from the JAM Orphanage. They support him through his struggles. *"They are like brothers and sisters to me."*

"If I am able to continue my studies at university I want to become a teacher. If I don't succeed with my secondary studies I will become a mechanic or a driver. I hope to become a teacher so that I can serve my country by educating children. However, I might fail because I don't get enough notebooks and I have to stay at home. I also dream of building a house on my father's land.

"Before the war I lived with my family and life was good. I was only five or six when the war broke out, but I remember that we were hiding in the forests in Kibuye. My mother was killed while I was with her. I was told that my father died the same day.

"I was travelling by bus when we were stopped and given some food before we were taken to Kigali. From Kigali I was brought to JAM Orphanage in Gitarama.

"I don't remember how I felt when the war was over. I just remember that I cried because my parents had died. I don't like to talk about the war because it reminds me of the people I lost. I don't think I will ever be able to forget the war, but I do try. I will not allow what happened to me to be a handicap in the future."

Vianney Mugemana
Age 14
Born in Gitwa, Bisesero.
Attends Esapan Secondary School, level 1.

Rebuilding their lives

Monique and Gaspard have four children; Manishimwe Joseph (six years), Iradukunda Joselyine (five years), Kwihangana Emmanuel (three years) and Ntivuguruzwa Joyeuse (five months).

Gaspard and Monique first met during the war whilst they were trying to escape the horror of death together, but were separated in the panic of escape. Later they were reunited at JAM Orphanage.

"After the war we both came to Gitarama as refugees. We were sent to Abundant Life International's Orphanage, and since I was already 24 years old I started working as a supervisor. When JAM took over I was employed and got a salary."

Monique adds: *"I got malaria and Gaspard helped me to get to hospital. I recovered and went back to school. Soon afterwards we fell in love and got married in 1995, one year after we came to Gitarama."*

Today Gaspard and Monique, who both lost families to the war, are living in Kibuye again. Said Gaspard: *"We felt that it was safe to go back home but we found that our house had been destroyed. I had to repair it so that my family could live there. I have some animals and I grow vegetables."* Gaspard's only income is from selling coffee to businessmen in Kibuye. *"I hope for a good future, but farming doesn't pay well. When I finish harvesting my coffee I will start looking for another job."*

Before the war Gaspard was a fisherman at Kivu Lake and his parents were farmers. The people of Kibuye loved each other, Hutus and Tutsis alike. There were many marriages between people from different tribes, but as the war progressed, the militia forced friends and neighbours to kill each other. It was then that they sought refuge in a church close by. But the militia arrived and killed nearly everybody hiding in the church. Fortunately Gaspard was hiding outside when this happened and was shocked by the killing in the church. He fled to Bisesero immediately.

In Bisesero he met up with Monique and many others. Unfortunately, the militia had already reached the village and intense fighting broke out for over a month. Gaspard and others were able to keep the militia away, but they came back...with guns. Many people died and the few that survived hid in the bushes until the French soldiers came for them. When they left Kibuye they met some RP soldiers in Rambora. The soldiers took them to the catholic church in Gitarama. Abundant Life International gathered all the children together and took them to the orphanage.

"People live in peace but it is different compared to before the war. Some families have members in prison while others lost family in the war. I am thankful for the good leadership we have in Rwanda today that tries to unite the people."

Gaspard Ntivuguruzwa
Age 32
Region: Karora, Murangara, Kibuye.
Works as a farmer on his own land.

Monique Mukarwema
Age 26
Born in Kibuye.
Region: Karora, Murangara, Kibuye.

Relative difficulties

After the war, Josephine's mother's cousin came to the orphanage to take her to her home and look after her. Josephine was happy to go with the cousin as she knew she was the only relative she had left after the war. However life with the cousin took an unexpected turn and Josephine began feeling differently towards the situation.

"I think that she doesn't love me because I am not her own daughter. I have sometimes had to leave school to look for materials because this lady doesn't look for the materials even though she sometimes has the means to get them for me. There is only one solution to this problem for me, and it is to get used to it because there is no other person that I can go and live with..."

Josephine is a high achiever in class but worries that the problems with her cousin could prevent her from finishing her studies in the future. She likes Rwanda because she was born there and one day hopes to travel and continue her studies abroad.

"I study hard because it will be helpful in my future. I would like to become either a teacher or a doctor, because I feel that these occupations contribute to the development of Rwanda. We have to study to develop our country and be able to replace the people who are doing jobs now, because Rwanda has not reached its potential."

Besides studying, Josephine likes to play ball games with her friends and values the fact that they can share things and be happy together.

"After the war the relationships between people were not good and are still affected today. When you come across families who are not happy to see you and mistreat you because you are not in the same ethnic group, you just have to be kind to them because we are created equal.

"I remember that when our parents died in the war you just followed someone else who could care for you, show you how to hide and where to hide. There was unity among the people who ran away together, because when they killed my relatives halfway through the war, I spent the rest of the time running behind a neighbour until the war was over and some people brought me to the orphanage.

"We were victims of the same things in the war and we needed to take care of each other because we were all in the same situation. After the war, the problem arose that nobody took care of you because there was no one who cared about you and people didn't have the means to take care of others. Even the adults missed their own children and lost their desire for parenting because of the war.

"I believe that people should avoid killing because the war only left orphans and destroyed things in Rwanda. When you are in a family, you work together to build up your future, but when you stay behind you have no aid and it is very difficult to have a good life."

Josephine Mukamukomeza
Age 14
Lives in Kinigi, Bisesero in Kibuye with her mother's cousin.
Attends P6 in Mumubuga Primary School.

Practical solution

Philbert, his younger brother and five sisters stay with his aunt in Gitarama. He is an ambitious young man who believes in the future of his country. Philbert's love for his family is evident and he is thankful for a second chance in life. Philbert and his family were separated during the war and only reunited when the war was finally over.

"My family ran to an area called Muchingi. The children were placed with different families while my parents ran back to our house. I haven't seen them since, but I was told that they were killed during the war. The family that I stayed with cared well for me. I had contact with my younger brothers and sisters because they were close by. I had not seen my older sisters and believed they had been killed as well.

"After about three weeks we had to leave the families because they were afraid that they would be found hiding us. We were brought to a refugee camp in Kapgai. After the war five of us went to the JAM Orphanage. My two older sisters heard that we were there and came to visit us. When school started my sisters asked Fred if they could take us home to my aunt. I was so happy to reunite with my family. Life was not the same in the orphanage. Even though we had everything we needed in the orphanage, we still missed our family."

Philbert is studying electricity in secondary school because he likes practical work. *"I don't want to sit in an office. Mostly I want to go to university to study electrical engineering. I hope that the Government fund can pay for my studies. I would like to repair and design big machines."*

"I am very happy with my life today. I go to school during the day and in the evenings I go to the cultural centre. Here we play volleyball, basketball and table tennis. There is also an Internet café and a library where I like to sit and read.

"I have not made any specific plans for my future after my studies. But if the development in my country continues I think that I will live well for the rest of my life."

Philbert Ndugu
Age 20
Born in Masango, Gitarama.
Attends Indangabure Secondary School,
level 5.

Head Boy

Alphonse has high aspirations for his life and dreams of a prosperous future. He has a strong character and it comes as no surprise that he is the head boy of his school. He wants to serve his country some day, because the Government is helping him make his dreams come true.

The Fund for Genocide Survivors (FARGE) is paying for his school fees, notebooks and pens. He takes care of any other costs besides these. He is concerned, however, about finances for next year to complete S6, his final school year. But he has faith that the Government will come through for him as they promised.

Getting a good education is Alphonse's first priority. **"I want to continue my studies after S6. If I get good marks I can attend university on a Government bursary. I have been first in my class since S4. I decided to study medicine in S3, because I have been interested in healing and treating the sick."**

Alphonse rarely thinks back on the war, but he misses his parents when he has to solve problems. He was very young at the time of the genocide but he remembers the fighting and people being killed everywhere. **"My younger brother and I had been hiding together throughout the war. For some reason I always believed that I would survive. In my heart I just held on to that hope.**

"The French troops arrived and they took us to the RP soldiers who went with us to Gitarama. Fred saved us from very bad conditions by starting the JAM Orphanage. He came with a car and they took all of us to the bishop's compound. We were given food and clothes. When the priests came back we moved to JAM in Shyogwe.

"The orphanage helped me a lot after the war, because my brother and I met people who were like new parents, who helped us to grow up and provided us with an education.

"I am happy when I think about my life – getting married and having children. I am also happy that my brother survived with me. His name is Ndengahimana Claver and he is currently in primary school. God has saved me from dying; given me a place to live, when I had no parents. He has done so many things that I cannot account for all of them."

Alphonse Ngarambe
Age 22
Born in Nyarutovu Bisesero.
Region: Mubuga, Kibuye.
In S5 in Ecoli de Sciences des Infirmaries in Mugonero, Ngoma in Kibuye.

"People should be eager to read and learn"

I live with my uncle (my father's brother) in the holidays, doing jobs like collecting firewood for cooking, doing some agricultural work, or looking after the cows. But my real hobby is reading.

"I like to read the Rwandan national newspaper in Kinya-rwanda or the notebooks from school or anything I can get, because you can learn many things you did not know before. People should be eager to learn, because it enables them to help themselves. Someone who studies and goes to university is able to get a good job, good salary and a good life. This is what I would like for my future.

"I remember that they killed my parents and all my relatives with spears and machetes within two days of the war starting. I was also wounded in my leg with a spear. After that I didn't feel anything because I thought that I would also die the following day. They used dogs to search for where we hid. Our clothes were destroyed in the forests and many people were running naked in the cold. While you were running, you saw people being killed behind you and when you hid in the bushes, others were being massacred around you.

"I don't like to talk about these things because it makes me feel sad, but I have friends from the orphanage that help me to be strong when I see them at school after the holidays. The genocide changed many things inside me.

"When I left JAM, I knew that things would be different because our areas were overgrown and everything was destroyed. I expected that life would be very bad, but I was happy to find out that my uncle was still alive. I have some problems because when someone is not your own parent, you can't tell him about all your needs. I have a problem with my eyes and get tears in my eyes when I read, but I can't tell my uncle to go and buy glasses for me, because I realise what kind of means he has. Even if I tell him about my problems he can't do anything about it. I feel bad about this, but I just bear it because I know that there is nothing else for me to do.

"I hope that I get the opportunity to finish my studies as I know that if I have to stop, there is no life for me in the future. I would like to study law to become a judge one day to avoid injustice. This is very important for me and for other people, because the war in Rwanda was caused by injustice and bad administration. If I get the opportunity to be an administrator, I can lead and do the things that the people need to progress. I have decided to be better than the leaders from before.

"By avoiding divisions between people and by following the good laws of the country, something like the genocide can be avoided. When people come to Rwanda, they realise what happened here and it is good, because everyone should know the causes and details of the genocide to help them avoid it happening to them."

Gaspard Nsabihimana

Age 18
Born in Bisesero.
Region: Bisesero, Kibuye.
Attends S1 in Esapan Secondary School.

"I wish I could have helped them all"

Niyigena has a mother now. Her name is Nzayisenga Alphonsine and she hopes that he continues to do well in his current class, finish his secondary studies and maybe study in the educational field one day. She has big dreams for him and will try her best to assist him in accomplishing them.

"Niyigena was always shy, even when he came here. We adopted him when the local authorities called a meeting and told us that there was an organisation coming and that people who felt encouraged to receive and adopt children into their homes should be encouraged to register as foster parents. I attended that and was very happy to receive Niyigena.

"We felt sorry for the children because there were many who live together and who don't get love and affection from families, like other children. It is good for a child to live in a family because he learns manners, culture and good education that helps him to grow into someone with a good personality who is able to help the family that has looked after him. Parents should also take children to school so that the teachers can give them an education that will enable them to work for the country.

"What the orphanage did for the children was that they gathered those who didn't have anybody to make life easier for them. They felt sorry for the children and enabled people who felt encouraged to receive children to help them. It was good to do something about the children, because they were wandering around in the bushes and streets."

Alphonsine appeals to people to open their hearts to the children and also consider that all children should have families and that God blesses those who bless others.

"God blesses you and you are also blessing your country if you help the children. There is no difference between Niyigena and my own children because they do everything together, regardless of what it is. They play together, eat together and whoever commits a mistake is punished in the same way as any other one of my children. Niyigena has truly become like family now.

"Orphans grow up with sorrow, because they don't know their parents. I feel sorry for them and if it wasn't for a lack of means, I wish that I could have helped all of them. Because people's hearts differ, some people care but others just don't..."

Niyigena Jean Damascene
Age: Eight years old.
Region: Kikoma, Ntongwe.
P1 primary school.

Mother and son reunited

Marcel had a happy life before the genocide. His father was a successful farmer and owner of a flourishing business. That all changed one evening when his father's friend from the Hutu tribe came to warn him that his tribe were out to kill the Tutsis. That night they all fled from their home to avoid any tribal conflict.

The next day Hutus arrived with an army of men and murdered women and children after breaking through the men's defence. Marcel's father was killed before his eyes. Later he met up with his mother and baby sister to bury his father. Tragedy hit once more; his older sister and a younger sister were murdered whilst trying to flee with their mother from the chasing troops.

"I think about the war sometimes. I think about how my father died and how my sisters died. I often think about our life before the war, how happy we were and what a good life we had together as a family. When I compare that life with the life I lead now, I get very sad and discouraged."

Both mother and son once again were separated when the French troops came to rescue everyone. Marcel was put on a different truck from his mother's and taken to the JAM Orphanage. He would only be reunited with his mother after many months apart.

"When the French people took us to Gitarama in September 1994 I was sent to the JAM Orphanage. I was told that the parents were sent to rural Kigali. From Gitarama my mother went back to Kibuye. She did not know if it was safe to go back so she had to leave me in the orphanage in case she would be killed when returning to Kibuye. I was not afraid because I was with other children from Gitarama. We all knew that our parents would come back to get us when it was safe to go home. We were trying to return to normal and forget about the war."

Today, Marcel stays with his mother and little sister in Mubuga. He helps his mother as best he can by working the land and milking the cows. They grow beans, maize, sorghum, cassava and sweet potatoes. They also have three cows and four goats. *"We rent a house in Mubuga, and my mother plans to go back to Bisesero when she can afford to build a new house."*

Marcel Nshimiyimana
Age 15
Born in Bisesero.
Region: Mubuga, Kibuye.
Attends Esapan Secondary School, level 2.

"Everybody that I live with are my friends"

Dorothee started going to school straight away when she first came to JAM. She was there for a year, until her mother's cousin came to the orphanage to take her home. The name of this lady was 'Mahoro' which means 'peace' in the Rwandan local language. However conditions in this family were not so peaceful because of the poverty they lived in.

"After some time, I saw that I had a problem if I stayed there because I didn't get school materials. My uncle decided to take me and helped me to continue with my second year in secondary school. Things are okay now. I am happy to stay with him because he treats me like one of his own children.

"When they took me from the refugee camp I was happy, but when I reached the orphanage my plan was always to leave and go to my place of origin. I wanted to see this place again because it had been a long time since we ran away. I felt bad because I was alone and I didn't have any relatives. The only comfort I had at this time was that I was in a group of children with the same problems.

"When the time came to leave, however, I was unhappy because of the bad living conditions of those that accepted us into their homes. My biggest wish after finishing my studies is to live the best life. The best life is to be able to provide everything you need yourself."

Memories of the war come back to her when she least expects it. She remembers how the killers came to kill the people wherever they found them and how she at times had to hide herself under the bodies to escape death.

"I have forgiven those who were involved because if I refuse to forgive, it will not restore my relatives to life. The most important thing now is for people to know that bad things happened here and they should not plan something like the genocide again.

"It might happen again, because it happened before, but I don't know what can be done to prevent something like it in future. On the other hand, I can say that everybody that I live with are my friends. I don't know if they like me, but as long as I like them, I feel peace inside me."

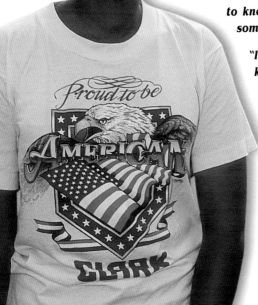

Dorothee Nyirahabimana
Age18
Lives in Gitesi in Kibuye with her uncle.
Attends S2 in Esapan Secondary School.

Life just got worse and worse

Christine's older sister and aunt are the only surviving family members she has. When she finishes her studies she would like to become a nurse and help her family that survived the war. Her family is very poor and Christine feels that her life was better in the orphanage.

"Since I had left the orphanage, my life just got worse and worse. I have been trying to go back to the orphanage to ask for help, but they told me that when a child is reunited with his family, they can't keep helping the child on the outside. I feel that I can stay in the home where I am living now, but I need to be helped by somebody."

Before the war Christine had three sisters and two brothers. Her father died soon after the war started and both her brothers were thrown into a river by the militia and her uncle was burned to death. Christine and her sister decided to separate.

"We said to one another that if one died the other one would at least survive. When the French came, my older sister went with them to Gitarama."

Christine stayed with a Hutu family and survived with them until the RPA arrived and the family had to flee to Congo. When Christine's older sister found out that she was alive, she sent someone to fetch her to go to the orphanage. She says that she was very happy and excited to meet her sister after the war. In her village there were only three other children who survived. She tries to keep communication with them, because she feels that there is usually unity among the children who survived, but is not often that you find them together.

Christine feels that people established the orphanages out of love because they did not want those who survived to become street children after the war.

"Some children have even become street children after they left the orphanage because of the bad conditions in the families they were united with. It can happen to anybody because of the general poverty among people."

She says that all these things are happening as a result of the war and if it were not for God, she would not be alive today. Now she feels that things are not too bad for her and that things are getting better.

"If I can say something about what happened to me, I can advise people not to keep thinking about what happened to them. They can stop division. It would be good to wipe this from our minds and live in peace with each other."

Christine would like to stay in Rwanda for the rest of her life because it is her country. She says that it makes her happy to live in her own country and that when she grows up, she can even be able to help her country by working for it.

Christine Nyiransengimana
Age 17
Born in Mwendo.
Region: Gisovu, Kibuye.
In S3 in Ecoli de Sciences des Infirmaries in Mugonero, Ngoma, Kibuye.

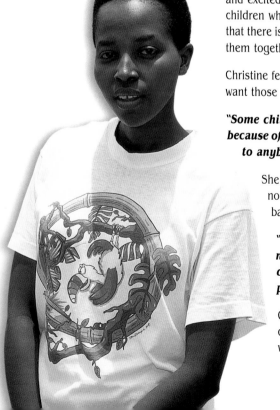

"One of my goals in life is to be a leader in Rwanda"

Alice loves every moment of school. Her favourite subjects are Psychology, Mathematics and Geography, and she strives for the best marks possible in her tests. She dreams of becoming a psychologist one day. She doesn't mind becoming a teacher, but would prefer to be a psychologist.

Alice misses her parents very much, especially when she faces problems and doesn't have anyone to turn to. Before the war, she lived in Kigali with her mother's sister who was married to the former Minister of Agriculture. He was instrumental in the downfall of the previous President and together with his wife and most of their children, was murdered at the outset of the war. Two of his surviving children fled the country and have never returned.

Alice was sent away to attend boarding school in Butare by her aunt. Many of the children at boarding school didn't have ID cards, so the militia didn't know which tribe they belonged to. To this day Alice is certain that this confusion amongst the militia saved them from being killed. Unfortunately, the headmaster was killed whilst buying food for the children. After his death the children had no option but to return to their families. Alice learnt that her aunt and the rest of her family had been killed whilst she was in boarding school, so had to stay with a teacher in Gitarama until the end of the war. Later she went to Birambo to look for her cousin who was her only surviving relative.

"My cousin and I went to the JAM Orphanage. I was happy to stay there because I could play with other children. I don't know what caused the genocide, but I've been told that the former Government planned to kill all the Tutsis when they found out that the Rwanda Patriotic Army wanted to attack them.

"I think it was the leaders who created division among people. To this day I don't see any unity amongst the people of Rwanda. In their hearts, they still hold things against each other. I believe in God because He protects me and helps me with my problems. People should love one another as God loves us. One of my goals in life is to be a leader in Rwanda and that is the main reason for me to continue my studies."

Alice Usabyimbabazi
Age 20
Born in Birambo.
Region: Julwe, Bisesero, Kibuye.
Attends Esapan Secondary School, level 6,
Teacher training section.

Foundation for the future

Emmanuel completed his secondary studies in 2001 and specialised in nursing. He would love to study further but at the moment he doesn't have the money to continue. He has already explored some of the options of sponsorship and Government scholarships and has realised that it would be easier for him to provide for himself. He is sceptical about his future if he is unable to continue his studies. He stays with his brother on his parents' land and looks forward to being independent one day.

"The Government has built a house for me, and if I have the basics to finish my house I can start to think about my future from this foundation. I cannot say that I really have hope for my future, because the first thing that will give me hope for the future is a foundation.

"I was in the JAM Fred Nkunda Orphanage for one year. When we arrived there, they put us with other children and within a few days they provided for any needs that we had and they put us in schools. The life in there was very nice and we were happy."

His brother used to come and visit him at the orphanage and one day asked the JAM administrators to allow Emmanuel to live with him. Emmanuel was happy to go home with his brother, and would not have left the orphanage for any other reason. He finished his secondary education while staying with his brother.

Emmanuel is still traumatised by the events of 1994, and often thinks about the war.

"I see and dream about what happened and it is not as if I am out of those situations, but as if I am still in the war, feeling afraid and isolated. If I had to talk about everything that happened to me in the war, it will fill an entire book. I feel that it is better to talk about those things, because sometimes when you talk about those things, you feel some satisfaction inside you – I don't know how to say it, but you feel that some bad feelings reduce and some things inside you change.

"Even though I have forgiven the killers, some of them don't understand how I could forgive. I cannot keep my forgiveness inside me, because as a Christian I am always taught how to forgive. I also know that only some people wanted to benefit from the property of others and got involved in the killing in 1994, while others were against the bad things that were happening.

"Many things in Rwanda changed because of the genocide. Health centres and schools were destroyed and the country lost many intellectuals. We are slowly approaching the level of development that we were at before the war and will slowly pass it when we reach it.

"I hope that development will even come to my village in the future and that foreign people will come and establish development projects from which we will all benefit. I would like to have a family one day when I have means and, if I get the opportunity to travel, I would also like it – not because I hate my country, but because you might have to look for a better life for the sake of your family. The quality of life of my family is important to me."

Emmanuel Rwigemera
Age 23
Lives in Bisesero in Kibuye with his brother.
Completed S6 in ESI School, Mugonero.

Toto Sylvere
Age 11
Lives with foster parents in rural Gitarama.
Attends P3 in Bweramvura Primary School.

Success story of cross-tribal fostering

A community leader in Bugarura has adopted Toto to be his son. It is one of the success stories of cross-tribal fostering. The happiness and love of this family towards Toto is inspiring and serves as an inspiration to a community in the process of reconciliation. Toto's foster father believes that children who grow up in families have a sense of purpose in the community. He has set an example in his area by being one of the first families to adopt a child of the other tribe.

Toto has his own little garden close to the house, where he grows his own flowers and crops. He says that when he saw other children who had gardens and were working in the lands he also decided that he wanted one. Toto likes studying and would like to become a medical assistant so that he can feel proud when people thank him for healing them.

Like many children who came from the sheltering environment of an orphanage, Toto was initially afraid and confused when he met his foster parents, but he says **"I became very happy in my heart when I arrived."**

Toto's foster father, Kubwimana Jean Baptiste, is happy that Toto has good dreams and goals for his future. He believes in community values and the importance of teaching Rwandan children a family culture, because it will help them to be beneficial to the country. Toto's father tells how Toto did not know how to cultivate crops or prepare a garden, but is learning from the family and is even able to look after a cow and can milk one himself. He also believes that educating children is the key to bringing development to their area.

"In the three years that I have been a leader we have had 60 children continuing with secondary studies because teachers and parents are friendly now and not dividing the tribes. Before 1996 people were afraid of meeting and coming together, but people eat and drink together and even give each other cows. The children in Rwanda have a future if the security that we have now lasts and they grow up with a good culture and good manners."

Jean Baptiste asks people and organisations to find out about the way of life in Rwanda so they can contribute and assist in establishing security in Rwanda. Then this country can be integrated into the rest of the world.

"I will teach children the rich culture of Rwanda"

Beatrice has high aspirations for her future: *"I would like to become a teacher because it will enable me to become independent and I will be able to serve my country by educating children. I am looking forward to teaching children who cannot read and write. I will teach them the rich culture of Rwanda and I will show them the importance of education."*

Beatrice faces many obstacles every day. She has been struggling to find a sponsor to help her with school material. She would love to attend university one day, but this will only happen if she succeeds in qualifying for a bursary from the Government. She is not despondent and believes that God is using people to bless her financially in order to achieve her goals.

Her father's cousin (her only surviving relative) looks after her. They have enough to eat each day but there is never any extra money to make other dreams come true. When the war broke out, Beatrice and her family fled to the former district office. The militia started shooting randomly at people and this is how the rest of her family died. Fortunately the bullets missed Beatrice and after the militia left, she and five other children fled.

"I hid until June when the French soldiers took us to the RP soldiers. They saw to it that we were placed with the JAM Orphanage. I was happy then because the staff took really good care of us. They taught me how to behave and how to live with people from different backgrounds.

"I don't know if I will ever be able to forget what I witnessed in the war. Before the war people were living together in peace, but today people are managing on their own and minding their own business."

Beatrice is thankful for many things that are a part of her life today. She's thankful that she survived the war and that God protected her then and now. She is filled with peace in her heart and has compassion for her fellow citizens. Beatrice loves people and it gives her great joy to develop friendships with a few very special people – people who understand her, bless her and love her.

Beatrice Uwimpuhwe
Age 19
Born in Rwamatamu, Nyagahinga, Kibuye.
Region: Cyika, Musenyi.
Attends Esapan Secondary School, level 4,
Teacher training section.

"My heart is getting softer all the time"

Berthilde is a sociable person and loves to have long conversations with her friends. Many of them were with her at the JAM Orphanage before they were all sent to families to live with. She enjoys being around people who make her happy and likes playing games and being a spectator to the game of soccer.

She is happy at school and enjoys studying each day. What she likes most about her school is that it is in the country with little around to distract her from studying. She would love to work in the big city one day and move to somewhere different besides the countryside. Her goal is to become a nurse.

"It would be good for me to treat people because many fall sick and have no treatment. I would like to study further in this direction so that I will know how to treat everybody. I would like to go university to study because when you don't go to school, you can't do anything for yourself.

"I am not really satisfied with my life because I lead a bad life. At home it is not very happy, but I accept it because there is no other thing I can do. My eldest sister is 20 years old. My other sister is 12 and my brothers are 18, 14 and eight. We all love each other and are happy to have each other because we all had the same parents.

Berthilde Uzayisenga
Age 16
Born in Gihuma.
Stays in a boarding school — College
St Jean Nyarusange.

"I am afraid of the future because my aunt who took care of us died, and our situation became worse. My grandmother takes care of us now. We rent land from one of the employees from the JAM Orphanage. My grandmother tries to use the land to support us but she is not very strong any more. There are also two other children that my grandmother has to support. We don't have enough food to eat.

"We all try to help her on the land and we also learn how to use the land. I like to learn how to use the land, but I would prefer to be a nurse one day to be able to help people.

"When I think that other children have lost everybody they had I am happy that I have brothers and sisters. My heart is getting softer and softer all the time. I want to have a good heart and be able to relax again. I try not to be sad, but when I start to think deeply about my life and when I remember my parents and the life we went through during the war, I go to play with my friends to help the sadness to go away.

"I wish that I could have a good life and nothing to disturb my complete freedom. A good life for me is to have peace without a problem. Maybe I will get peace in future, but in Rwanda the peace is not enough. I cannot be happy when the country is suffering."

Abbreviations

RPA — Rwandan Patriotic Army - The army of the Rwandan Patriotic Front

IRC — International Rescue Committee

ICRC — International Committee of the Red Cross

NGO — Non-Governmental Organisation